Greece

If you were to measure the media attention received by any one country over the course of a decade – say, the ten years since 2010 – not many could boast the level of coverage focused on Greece, and this despite being relatively small geographically and economically. Likewise, few countries are portrayed in such a variety of ways, depending on one's perspective. Let's play this game together – with a hefty dose of generalisation: viewed from the east, Greece is historically the enemy (what the Turks know as 'Independence', the Greeks call the 'Catastrophe'); looking from the Middle East or the north-African shore of the Mediterranean, it is a place that people are desperate to reach; from the west, it is seen as an awkward relative best kept at arm's length ('We are not Greece' is a common refrain in some parts of Europe); if you come from the north, Greece is the grave of the European Union; but, if you live in Greece, the country is the cradle of Western civilisation. It is also a sacrificial victim at the mercy of powerful interests if you are a dove, while from a hawkish perspective it is irredeemably corrupt and dragged down by bureaucracy. Whatever your angle, though, it seems impossible not to have an opinion. This is what happens when you're pushed on to the world stage: stories are drowned out by 'news', emotions trump facts and personalities take the place of actual people. The team who worked on this volume was no different; everyone had their own view on Greece – and, guess what, each was different. We did our best to ignore our preconceptions in our efforts to restore dignity to stories, facts and people; you, as readers, will decide whether we have been successful. One thing is certain, however, after working on this we all tried to slip back into our old preconceptions – but we realised they no longer held.

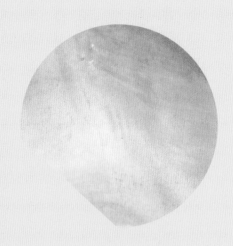

Contents

The photographs in this issue were taken by the documentary photographer **Pietro Masturzo**. After graduating in international relations from the University of Naples, he devoted himself to photography and reportage, focusing on social and political issues. He has worked in the Middle East, Southeast Asia, Europe and North Africa, documenting wars and human-rights violations. His photographs have appeared in numerous magazines and newspapers, including *L'Espresso*, *Corriere della Sera*, *La Stampa*, *Internazionale*, *The New Yorker*, *Le Monde* and *Vanity Fair*. His work has been recognised with numerous awards, including the prestigious World Press Photo of the Year in 2010 for his image of Iranian women shouting their disapproval of Mahmoud Ahmadinejad's election as president from a Tehran rooftop.

THE PASSENGER

For explorers of the world

Coming in
Autumn 2020

BRAZIL

In this volume: the road that dissects the Amazon, the TV tycoon who shaped Brazilian history, the neo-charismatic community that is winning the hearts (and wallets) of Brazilians, politicised samba dancers, idealist narcos and much more ...

Paperback | 978-1-78770-241-7

TURKEY

In this volume: the failed coup that was thirty years in the making, the rise of femicide in New Turkey, the flooding of a 12,000-year-old town, the political satirist resisting censorship, the communist mayor, business à la Turque, protest rap and much more ...

Paperback | 978-1-78770-242-4

Greece in Numbers

NO SLACKING

Number of hours worked annually

(OECD countries)

1. Mexico ////////////////////////// — 2,250

2. South Korea ////////////////////// — 2,070

3. Greece ████████████████ — **2,035**

4. India /////////////////////// — 1,980

14. USA /////////////////// — 1,781

24. UK ////////////////// — 1,676

SOURCE: OECD

WORKING MOTHERS

Greece is last in Europe

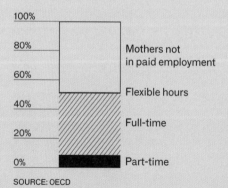

- Mothers not in paid employment
- Flexible hours
- Full-time
- Part-time

SOURCE: OECD

WORKFORCE

Population: 10.8M / Emigrants: 200,000

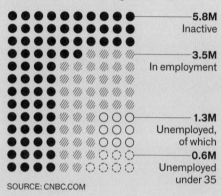

5.8M Inactive

3.5M In employment

1.3M Unemployed, of which

0.6M Unemployed under 35

SOURCE: CNBC.COM

FOREIGN CASH

'Golden Visas' issued to foreigners who invest in property

—— Greece ······ Portugal –– Spain –·– USA

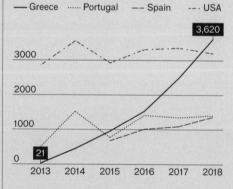

SOURCE: IMIDAILY.COM

SOCIALISING

(OECD and selected countries)

▇ Women   ////// Men

1. France
131
134

3. Greece
122
134

20. UK
78
80

29. USA
60
63

SOURCE: OECD

OLIVE OIL

Annual
consumption
per head
(litres)

❶

Greece (20l)

❷

Spain (14.2l)

❸

Italy (11.3l)

❹

Portugal (8l)

❺

Syria (4.9l)

SOURCE: INT. OLIVE COUNCIL

A NATION OF SHIPOWNERS

1st

in the world for
vessel ownership

+4k

Vessels

108.2

Total value
in billions
of dollars

SOURCE: VESSELS VALUE

HYPERACTIVE

Number of times
people have sex
each year

**1. Greeks
164**

2. Brazilians
145

3. Russians/Poles
145

4. Indians
130

SOURCE: STATISTA

A PROUD PEOPLE

'We might not be perfect, but our culture is superior to others.'

Percentage of people who broadly agree with this statement

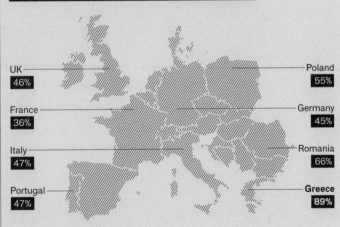

UK
46%

France
36%

Italy
47%

Portugal
47%

Poland
55%

Germany
45%

Romania
66%

Greece
89%

SOURCE: PEW RESEARCH CENTER

The Mythbuster

1

'Ancient Greek has nothing to do with the modern Greek language.'

Greek was never subject to the same sort of hiatus that gave rise to the Romance languages after the demise of Latin. Including its dialects and the diaspora down the ages, Greek is spoken by 13.5 million people and is the oldest attested living European language. It has evolved, of course: simplification of the grammar, lexicon introduced by periods of foreign control (Turkish, Italian, Venetian, French ...) and phonetic changes. The language has also suffered the effects of purist tendencies aiming to bring it closer to an idealised past: the Attic dialect of classical Athens as studied in school. Western philology originated during the Renaissance, when people once again began to study the classical language, but, in the meantime, Greek had been transformed and had almost entirely ceased to be spoken in the West. The discrepancy between written and spoken Greek widened until the 'language question' emerged in the late eighteenth century. Serious enough to cause protests and deaths, this dispute pitted supporters of *katharevousa*, 'purified' Greek, against champions of *dimotiki*, the 'language of the people', which has been the official language since 1976.

ELISABETTA GARIERI
Translated by Alan Thawley

Debunking stereotypes
and cliches

'The sirtaki is a traditional Greek dance.'

The sirtaki was choreographed in 1964 for Michael Cacoyannis's film *Zorba the Greek,* based on the masterpiece of the same name by the novelist Nikos Kazantzakis. Driven by the film's global success, 'Zorba's Dance' became a tourist icon and began to be taught in Greece because of the high demand. The melody is a composition by Mikis Theodorakis, inspired by the *Kritika syrta* (Cretan *syrta*) he had heard at traditional *panigiria* festivals in Chania. According to the director, the name 'sirtaki' was chosen at random, based on the term *syrtos,* deriving from *syro,* meaning to pull, which references various traditional dances with a 'dragging' step. The steps of the sirtaki are hopped, however, and were inspired by the *hasapiko,* the ancient dance of the butchers of Constantinople and Macedonia. It seems that the sirtaki was choreographed by the dancer Giorgos Provias – who taught the actor Anthony Quinn along with his colleague Dimos Ambatzoglou – but was forced to leave the shoot before the end of the film and did not enjoy the fame he deserved.

2

A Sign of the Times

THOMAS TSALAPATIS
Translated by Konstantine Matsoukas

Sixty-three people – among them Dimitris-Richardos Mylonas, the 51-year-old owner of the chain of pawnshops that bears his name – were arrested in a police operation in Attica, Volos and Thessaloniki, mounted to dismantle two criminal organisations engaged in gold trafficking. Known from his TV commercials, Richardos is owner of more than thirty stores.

'They legitimised the profits of their criminal activities through the acquisition of property such as expensive homes, land, vehicles and boats, the expansion of businesses and so on, through specific processes that met the three stages of legalisation required by law: placement, layering and incorporation,' the police press officer said.

The financial losses to the state amounted to many millions of euros.

For the period from June to October 2018 the police estimate state losses from gold trafficking at close to €1 million for each group. Evidence points to networks that involve, among other things, forged invoices, fake winning lottery tickets, Chinese clothing wholesalers, as well as shares in companies and property and so on. Dozens of shops selling and buying gold, jewellery shops and silversmiths' workshops in the centre of Athens, in the suburbs and in the area around the capital seem to have been involved, directly or indirectly, in the activities of two large organisations that exported gold illegally to Turkey in return for enormous profits.

Emblematic of the economic crisis, shops with huge signs announcing – or warning – 'I BUY GOLD' have been synonymous in recent years with exploitation, despair and hopelessness. In 2010–12, 947 such operations came into being. Their actual number could be two or three times higher than that, but this remains essentially unknowable since a great many operate under the radar. Yet, even in the legal ones, the bad practice and irregularities in their documentation, transactions and receipts are widespread.

In the midst of the anxiety generated by specialised economic indexes, diagrams and unfamiliar fiscal terms, gold and hard cash represent a return to a more archaic mode of exchange, seemingly safer and certainly more immediate. This regression is observable during every crisis, and it was the case in 2008 when similar operations were starting up in Greece, Spain and Italy. Every part of the Mediterranean has its own black-market agents and operations (often found on the same street, next to or across the road from one another). One always sees the same thing: a bullet-proof window with the aesthetics of the cheapest of cheap advertising and the aggressive yellow of gold (or bile) dominant. Capital letters and exclamation marks everywhere – and a security camera overlooking an office furnished with the understated simplicity of a funeral parlour: a desk somewhere in the back; a clerk wearing a look of indifference. Above street level, high up, signs blink on and off with the noise of despair. Pawnshops and moneylenders, licensed by the local police, buy goods at 15–40 per cent of their actual value. Except this is no purchase but rather setting a price on despair. The currency is need. Wedding rings and baptismal crosses, watches and jewellery, everyday mementoes and heirlooms are sent off to some illegal smelter and then stashed somewhere abroad.

In their midst is Mr Richardos, his name gleaming like a gold tooth on the signs of his shops. 'Come and join us in Athens and all over Greece,' the commercial urges. 'Richardos Pawnbrokers: the solution to the crisis.' Indeed, for the traffickers in despair, all this was a solution or, better, an opportunity. If you think about it, Richardos and all the gold-plated crew of pawnbrokers and moneylenders are really a lumpen version of the 'golden boys', those young whizz-kids of international finance. Illegal, underground and well connected, they reap gains from generalised defeat, they wish for a deepening of the collective wound, they wash their hands in the tears of those around them. Cynicism becomes a daily transaction. A high-street version of the companies that have taken on the collections of red debts and of the financial circles that precipitated the crisis. Of the legitimate pawnbrokers who determine the economy and its indexes, placing bets on failure and extinction.

And the more the times change, the more the slogan remains: 'The black marketeer of the past, the pawnbroker of today: scum for all time.'

Theatre of Crisis

GRAZIANO GRAZIANI
Translated by Alan Thawley

T heatre in a Greek context is influenced by the country's indissoluble
link to ancient drama and its origins in Greece. And since Greek tragedies
are the archetype of theatre and inform
Western culture as a whole, this casts a
very long shadow over the present. But it
would be an enormous mistake to reduce
today's Greek theatre to the glories of the
past because, thanks to the economic crisis
that has hit the country, theatre in Greece
is currently emerging as a particularly
interesting source of experimentation.

Like other European countries, in recent
years Greece has produced a number of
figures of international stature who have
swelled the ranks of a certain type of theatrical aristocracy. These artists are present at
all the major European events and have laid
the first foundations of a shared theatrical
heritage for this strange entity that is the
EU, with all its different nations, languages
and literary traditions. Notable examples
are Theodoros Terzopoulos and Dimitris
Dimitriadis, the first an internationally
renowned director and the second a
playwright and poet. They represent the
theatre of major productions, with impressive staging and scripts – in the case of
Dimitriadis – that embrace the modern and
contemporary lyrical tradition. However,
the most interesting seeds of renewal are
coming from the younger, more underground theatre, in terms both of practices
and aesthetics. For example, in 2011, at the
height of the economic crisis, when public
funding for culture was cut so savagely that
the relevant ministry was closed down and
cultural spaces were shutting on a daily
basis, the Embros Theatre in Athens was
set up as a squatted, self-managed operation. Also, in recent years a number of
contemporary plays have used language
that, while direct, is laden with symbolic
interpretations in an attempt to transform
the political condition of a debt-laden population and the difficult relationship with
Europe into fuel for dramatic writing that
attempts to create an epic out of the everyday, inevitably drawing on the structures
of myth.

This approach can be seen in the plays
of Giannis Tsiros and Alexandra K*. In his
play *Wild Seed*, written in 2013 and shown
for four consecutive seasons, Tsiros sets up
an improbable investigation conducted on
a beach into the disappearance and possible murder of a German tourist. The suspect is Stavros, a pig farmer who runs an
illegal souvlaki stand and whose daughter
had a brief fling with the missing man. In
her revelatory 2018 work *Revolutionary
Methods for Cleaning Your Swimming Pool*,
Alexandra K* presents a semi-serious
inter-generational conflict, in which a
father builds a villa with a swimming pool
to provide his children with economic security, but he has no planning permission,

and the methods he uses are the same as those that have left the country in such a mess: the villa becomes the backdrop for a clash between a younger generation who have studied, are steeped in international culture, devoted to art and at ease with German friends (the Germans again) and a father obsessively clinging to his roots and driven by money. In spite of this, he comes to embody the discontent of a country that has been sold out and even goes so far as to declare secession from Greece, founding a micronation in his own home in protest at his people's sense of confusion and lost sovereignty. The complex relationship with Germany, the heavy burden passed down from parents to children, economic and cultural corruption, the sell-off of a country that transformed itself into Europe's resort in order to avoid collapse and the constant flow of large numbers of young people who prefer to emigrate and abandon Greece to its destiny of decline: these are the striking elements, both symbolic and highly concrete, of these experimental plays that attempt to tell the story of present-day Greece. The same thinking underpins an Italian experiment written by the duo Deflorian/Tagliarini: the starting point for their play *We're Leaving So You Don't Have to Worry Anymore* was the disturbing opening of a novel by Petros Markaris – the popular Greek crime writer, whose article on Greek eating habits appears on page 67 of this issue of *The Passenger* – in which four elderly women whose state benefits have been cut opt to commit suicide rather than face the struggles of old age without resources or dignity. The economic crisis has turned out to be a powerful trigger for a new European theatre, whether it originates in Greece or refers to Greece as a symbol and a sacrificial victim on the altar of the neoliberal religion.

Athens:
A Palimpsest
of Perspectives

A view of the Acropolis
in Athens at night.

Journalist Nikos Vatopoulos takes us
on a walk to explore the buildings and
different eras of Athens, a city of many
faces – both ethnic and architectural –
in which change is the only constant.

NIKOS VATOPOULOS
Translated by Konstantine Matsoukas

15

There are times when I feel like a traveller of old standing awestruck before ancient ruins, the allure of which has beguiled me from a young age. I would try to capture the sense of glory and loss in a way that was almost existential. When I was young, in the first decades after the Second World War, although Athens did have many abandoned buildings, the 'ruins' referred more to the fragments of an ancient past, lost in time under layers of successive generations, rather than to the debris of a more recent urban landscape.

I was born in Athens at a time when everything was changing. The new world was emerging at breakneck speed and any comment in praise of the near past possessed an aura of romantic naivety. The idea of a new, modern Greece reborn after the disastrous 1940s was irresistible, intoxicating and, despite mistakes and blunders, has pretty much survived into the first years of the twenty-first century.

I have taken photographs of Athens ever since I was an adolescent, when, still at school, I would take note of its old houses at intersections or squeezed between six-storey apartment blocks. I photographed them – maybe artlessly – but in the spirit of a collector gathering prized possessions. There was a bond there. But, because of the economic crisis, daily life in Athens started to change around 2010, and I felt myself changing alongside it, aging with my city, experiencing its transformations like a sore on my body or as if the greying of my hair were suddenly accelerating. I opened my eyes and saw my city anew. The buildings that were modern in the 1960s, now I saw them as aged as I was. I started regarding the keepers of old Athens with different eyes. Found in the centre but in much greater concentrations in the suburbs, the ruins of the noble city stood like mummified royalty. They became my new and much-loved friends.

Street by street, I started to record them. The residential areas, which have played a part in Greek life since the nineteenth century, were full of houses that felt unwanted. They had survived the successive waves of demolition, mainly after 1955, that had transformed the look and scale of the city. It would be overly simplistic to suggest that the lack of care given to these early-twentieth-century homes, with their trademark Athenian style, was purely a result of the economic crisis. That is only part of the story. These abandoned homes of old Athens are in the state they are in also as a result of years of lack of appreciation as well as legal complications and issues around inheritance. Although many have been granted preservation orders and are under the legal protection of the state, they stand there in ruins. Several have collapsed. They are a spectacular and dramatic sight.

I wonder if those who visit Athens and know about the city mainly through their imaginations, through literature and dreams rather than through experience, pay attention to such buildings. For Greeks,

NIKOS VATOPOULOS graduated in sociology from the Deree American College in Athens and specialised in European studies at the University of Reading, UK. Since 1988 he has worked for the Greek newspaper *Kathimerini*, writing mainly about Athens; between 2007 and 2014 he was editor of the Art and Culture section. His books include *Facing Athens* (Potamos Publications, 2008) and *Walking in Athens* (Metaichmio, 2019), a selection of articles from his Sunday column. As well as being a journalist, Nikos Vatopoulos is also a photographer and organises walking tours focusing on the architecture of Athens.

including me and most of my generation, the idea of a modern Athens is one that combines triumph and grief. Generations of Athenians grew up with the sense that this city had paid the price for its post-war prosperity with the loss of that sense of scale and harmony that were the mark of Athens up to around 1955–1960, despite the great social inequalities and contradictions found there. Those born after 1970 have embraced the notion of a thwarted Athens.

Looking over the city from its historic hills, the Acropolis or Lycabettus, one realises just how big Athens is. Fortunately, the population has stabilised since 1990 – although it is impossible to know exact numbers because of the large number of foreign migrants. And you cannot understand contemporary Athens without taking immigration into consideration, as it has transformed life in the city. Athens had been relatively homogeneous racially up to 1990 and the arrival of the first waves of migrants, mainly from the Balkans, Poland and the former Soviet Union. More recently, and for a number of years, migrants from Asia and Africa have colonised whole areas in the centre as well as the old middle-class neighbourhoods.

To make sense of Athens – including its scattered, forgotten houses – one needs to consider the cycles of population change after 1830. The view over Athens from the Acropolis often resembles a silvery-white sea of densely packed buildings, most constructed after 1950. In one sense, Athens is a triumph of cubist modernism or the vindication of Le Corbusier on a grand scale. Visitors need to give Athens time if they are to understand it. With its very particular profile, it is one of the most impressive examples of urban experimentation anywhere in Europe. Although it would be easy to interpret its post-war spread as a reflection of the population's mass convergence on the city, that view is restrictive. Athens was reborn in the 1830s in a climate of European romanticism during the period of the birth of nations. Greece is a young state, the same age as Belgium, but older than Italy, Germany or any of the Balkan countries.

Looking at photographs of Athens from the mid-nineteenth century, it is hard to believe that it is the same city we see today. Most of the nineteenth-century private homes have been replaced by newer and, in many cases, better buildings, as Athens has been under construction constantly. The small, idiosyncratic, belle époque city hosted the first modern Olympic Games in 1896, a time when Greece was a small nation, poor and with inadequate infrastructure, yet with the ambition to express the spirit of the new Hellenism. Ever since that time – a period that took in the acme of the city's urbanisation but also bankruptcy, Greek pride as well as humiliation (such as the disastrous war of 1897 against the Ottoman Empire) in an environment of pronounced nationalism – Athens continued to grow as a neoclassical capital. Today one can still see public buildings from that era but very few private homes. The shells of the houses one finds today in the city's residential suburbs date from 1900 to 1940. The earlier city, small but with the attitude of a national capital, had adopted neoclassicism as its architectural style – a natural consequence of the 1834 declaration that Athens would become the capital of the new Greek kingdom. With young Otto – the son of Bavaria's passionately philhellene King Ludwig I – as its first monarch the small town was organised as a modern city along clearly classicist lines. Although modest in scale, Athens exerted enormous appeal both for the Greeks of the diaspora – who saw in the new capital the cradle of the nation's rebirth – and for

A tyre shop in Piraeus.

One of the many run-down houses in central Athens.

A map by P.W. Forchhammer showing
that in the mid-nineteenth century
Athens was still a village with
a population of only a few thousand.

the cultivated European public as a whole. The Acropolis and other monuments of classical antiquity were scattered around the nucleus of the old city over a wide area that was as yet free of construction.

Today it is hard to discern the classical landscape. However, around the 2004 Olympic Games a project was initiated for the integration of archaeological sites in central Athens, which created a pedestrianised zone around the Acropolis, and the walk from the Ancient Agora (a public space in classical Athens) to the Acropolis Museum has become one of the most celebrated in the city. The Athenian landscape is, for the most part, buried beneath the modern streets and buildings, but it emerges unexpectedly at points and elicits powerful associations. There is the enchanting profile of the ancient hills facing the Acropolis in the neighbourhood of Thissio as well as the area around the river Ilissos, which was covered over in the 1950s. These poetic interludes, with their almost pagan associations, among the trees of Attica – pine, laurel, arbutus – and the smooth rocks, the natural soil and the wildflowers in spring and autumn, are a reminder of the city that was and, *mutatis mutandis*, could be born again.

They also offer a sharp contrast to the often smothering density of the buildings in Athens, with its narrow streets and few open spaces. Yet there, in that compact urban network, is to be found the genetic material of one of the most fascinating cases of urban rebirth in Europe.

When I walk through the city centre I see, as if on a screen, the buildings that were there fifty or sixty years ago, the ones that lent an air of real class to streets great and small. In Athens, with a few exceptions, properties and city blocks are small: Athens reflects its history of small ownership that, like small-scale businesses, accounted for most of the city's urbanisation, at least during the long period between 1840 and 1980. Building fever was everywhere until the 2009 economic crisis, which shone a light on chronic problems in the Greek economy and in the wider society.

From the earliest days of the modern city there was a desire to create a capital worthy of the name. Numerous mansions were designed to lend Athens an air of grandeur – especially after 1870, when a concerted effort was under way to modernise Greek society. Large neoclassical buildings were gradually erected – from the university, by Danish architect Christian

Hansen in 1842, to the nearby Academy of Athens (considered one of the most elegant examples of public architecture anywhere in the world), completed in the 1880s and based on plans by the architect Theophilus Hansen, Christian's brother and the more widely acclaimed of the two in Europe. The entrance is adorned by statues of Athena and Apollo on lofty columns, and the relief work, with designs by Hansen himself, shows the level of the capital's ambitions.

But the building of the Athens Academy is also a reminder of the international networks of ideas and people that reached nineteenth-century Athens through the interchange of ideas and synergies with the rest of Europe. The building was financed by the Greek baron, Simon Sinas, a member of the powerful Greek community in Vienna (as was Nikolaus Dumba, who financed the erection of the Wiener Musikverein). It was Sinas who engaged Theophilus Hansen, then practising as an architect in Vienna (where, among other buildings, he also designed the Austrian parliament, which resembles the Athens Academy, although it is more severe in tone). Hansen arrived in Athens with his student, Ernst Ziller, a Saxon architect who would remain in Greece, become naturalised and marry a Greek. Ziller introduced his own architectural style, a mix of neoclassicism and Renaissance, erecting approximately five hundred buildings in Greece.

All this is relevant to an understanding of contemporary Athens. Ziller had a particular aesthetic sense, using a range of references such as caryatids, Pompeiian red pigment, mannerist staircases and sphinxes in marble and clay. He imposed a distinctive style on the city and had a great many followers. Everyone knows Ziller in Greece; his name is part of modern Greek mythology.

Ziller may have had a wealthy clientele and personal friendships with the indefatigable German Heinrich Schliemann, excavator of Troy, and with King George I – of the Danish House of Glücksburg, which replaced the Bavarian dynasty in Greece in 1863 – but his spirit impacted the whole of society and affected even the less affluent areas of Athens; in fact, one truly moving aspect of the city today is the continued visible presence of the neoclassical built environment in working-class neighbourhoods. A few houses have had preservation work done; others, however, belong to the long list of abandoned buildings in the city. Those saved from the sweeping reconstruction of the post-war period stand witness to a silent urban rebirth that took place before the war. The one- or two-storey, neoclassical working-class house of Athens attests to a particular cultural value. Gradually, after about 1910 or 1915, and following the effects of the modernising reforms introduced by Eleftherios Venizelos when he was prime minister (1910–20 and 1928–33), neoclassicism, with its evolved aesthetic and morphological idiom, began to recede. Initially, space was made available for hybrid aesthetic experimentation with the romantic outgrowths of eclecticism, and, gradually at first, the influence of art nouveau and, following 1925, art deco became more evident. After 1930 this dovetailed well with the vanguard of the modernist movement.

In Athens, and everywhere in so-called 'Old Greece' (which is to say the southern part of modern Greece before its expansions north in 1881 and again in 1912–13), the hold of neoclassicism as the heritage style of the early years of the modern nation proved particularly tenacious. For many decades the Greek home was the neoclassical home, identified with Greece's urbanising and Europeanising tendencies as well as with an often passionate spirit of patriotism that sustained the 'Great Idea'

The façade of a building in central Athens.

THE PASSENGER Nikos Vatopoulos

– the move towards a gradual unification of those areas in the Balkans, the Aegean, Asia Minor and Cyprus with large communities of Greek and Greek-speaking populations. The Great Idea was a continuation of the War of Independence (the Revolution of 1821 as it is called in Greece), and it survived until 1922, when the Greek armed forces suffered a humiliating defeat in Asia Minor following a turnaround of the international climate against Greece's ambitions but also the insistence of the Greek government in continuing the war.

For Greeks, 1922 was the year of the 'Great Catastrophe' and the great fire in the most prosperous city in the Near East, Smyrna (modern Izmir). This disaster, which was critical in the formation of the modern Greek state, led to the exchange of populations between Greece and Turkey in accordance with the Lausanne Treaty of 1923. We need to take this into account if we are to understand modern Athens, as over a million refugees came from Turkey to settle permanently in Greece, and the capital, along with Piraeus, took in hundreds of thousands of homeless people, uprooted from a place in which there had been a Greek presence for centuries. The geopolitical map had changed for ever, as had the fates of many thousands of people, affecting Greece and Athens economically, socially and culturally. It is not something widely known or understood outside the country's borders, but for Greeks it is as pivotal an event as were the German Occupation and the civil war in the 1940s. Both these historical chapters impacted decisively and irreversibly on the development of Athens from a small, charming, neoclassical city into a metropolis.

The arrival of the refugees from Asia Minor in 1922–3 forced the rapid expansion of the city, with all the attendant problems

The History of Modern Greece

enacted. The country comprises Attica, the Cyclades, Euboea and the Peloponnese, with a total population of around 800,000.

1821
The insurrection against the Ottomans begins in the Peloponnese. This revolt organised by the secret society Filiki Eteria (Society of Friends) comes to an end with the intervention of the alliance of three great powers (Great Britain, France and Russia), who defeat the Ottomans and their Egyptian allies at the Battle of Navarino (1827).
The Greek people's struggle for liberation, marked by massacres committed by the Ottomans, strikes a chord in Europe, and Greek friendship committees spring up in numerous places. The following year the first constitution of independent Greece is

1832
The London Convention signed by Great Britain, Russia, France and Bavaria proclaims Otto von Wittelsbach King of Greece.

1834
The capital moves from Nafplio to Athens.

1863
George I, son of the future king of Denmark, is named King of the Hellenes.

1864
Great Britain cedes the Ionian Islands to Greece.

but also many positive opportunities. Suburbs sprang up, some of them improvised and with insufficient infrastructure but some properly planned and with new styles of residential buildings. All of this required the modernisation of the water facilities, the establishment of green spaces on the outskirts and the construction of working-class districts. Athens became a populous city for the first time at the end of the 1920s, and, with the demise of the Great Idea, it emerged with a new role: the capital of a homogeneous state with a dynamic population.

It can be hard to appreciate that many Athenian suburbs came into being at that time. Before, the suburbs functioned primarily as resorts, either to the north – Kifissia, for example, with its abundant greenery and running water (popular since Roman times) – or to the south, Neo Faliro, with its hotels and beaches. The axis of the mountains and the sea is key to understanding how Athens works and how Athenians live their lives. It is possible to swim at well-maintained beaches fifteen or twenty kilometres from the centre of the city, while up in the mountains – well forested despite the many wildfires that rage in the summer – there are opportunities for hiking and hill climbing, picnicking and other leisure activities (one fine example of which is the Tatoi Palace, the former royal estate).

Athens had already started to move away from neoclassicism by the milestone year of 1922. Experiments in form and function were slow to reach Greece in those days, but the urban cityscape felt the influence of international trends sooner or later, mainly through the work of Greek architects who studied in Germany or France. Up to the beginning of the twentieth century Athens had managed to articulate its own aesthetic

1881
Following the call issued by the great powers at the Berlin Congress (1878) for the Ottoman Empire to redraw its borders in favour of Greece, the Ottomans give up Thessaly and Arta in Epirus.

1897
The Greco-Turkish war ends with the defeat of Greece.

1910–13
Eleftherios Venizelos's government passes a constitutional reform and, in the aftermath of the First and Second Balkan Wars, under the terms of the treaties of Bucharest and London, gains Thessaloniki, Ioannina, Chios, Samos, Mytilene, Crete and the islands of the Aegean (with the exception of the Dodecanese) for Greece.

1914
Greece enters the First World War on the side of the Triple Entente.

1922
The Greco-Turkish war, which had begun in 1919, ends with the Catastrophe of Asia Minor.

4 August 1936
After years of political instability, General Ioannis Metaxas establishes a dictatorial regime inspired by Italian fascism. He imagines a 'third Hellenic civilisation' that, under his protection, would combine the virtues of Greece's first pagan civilisation and the second Byzantine Christian civilisation.

'Athens became a populous city for the first time at the end of the 1920s, and, with the demise of the Great Idea, it emerged with a new role: the capital of a homogeneous state with a dynamic population.'

and architectural idiom based on the principles of neoclassicism, albeit with a fair degree of variation depending on the building's intended use and the owner's financial circumstances. Athenian neoclassicism (which was also adopted in many cities in southern Greece – Ermoupoli, the capital of Syros, for example) is a distinct branch of international neoclassicism with a full and well-organised palette in its aesthetic paintbox. With the exception of certain mansions in the centre that belonged to a wealthier class of owner – and which featured a more international style of classicism – the typical Athenian house,

whether aimed at the middle class or working class, was usually of one or two storeys and almost always had a garden or yard. Morphologically, it was distinguishable by a frieze with clay antefixes, decorative pillars beside the windows and marble supports under the balconies, which also featured elaborate iron railings.

The neoclassical house has passed into the modern mythology of Athens. For Greeks it has acquired sacrosanct status, maybe because this heritage was historically so badly served. It is estimated that approximately 75 per cent of pre-Second World War homes in Athens were demolished after

28 October 1940
To balance the German presence in the Balkans, Mussolini, who is sure of an easy victory, decides to invade Greece. He issues Metaxas with an ultimatum ordering him to agree to the occupation, but the Greek leader refuses. Italian troops enter Greece but are driven back into Albanian territory.

April 1941
The Germans invade Greece. The first resistance actions begin after a few weeks, and the National Liberation Front (EAM) is established.

1946
After being freed from occupation the country descends into a bloody civil war between the partisan forces and supporters

of the monarchy, which is restored following a controversial referendum.

21 April 1967
A long period of political instability, with significant foreign interference, leads to the coup that installs the military junta formed by Georgios Papadopoulos, Stylianos Pattakos and Nikolaos Makerezos. The regime of the Colonels begins.

22 September 1971
The funeral of the poet and Nobel literature laureate George Seferis turns into a demonstration against the regime.

1973
Following a referendum held under martial law, the new republican constitution

hostilities ceased. However, the demolition of nineteenth-century houses had already begun in the inter-war years, although it was not that widespread because the circumstances were different.

Between the wars something noteworthy took place. The demolition of old homes liberated plots of land in the centre of the city on which the first modern buildings could be erected. It is perhaps not widely known that Athens is home to an impressive array of modernist buildings, mainly private, although there are a few public ones, too. They are either pure Bauhaus or in a more urban style, with elements of art deco. Hundreds of apartment blocks were built between 1932 and 1940, at which point Greece was sucked into the Second World War.

I often think how unimaginative the promotion of Athens can be – and especially the Athens of the inter-war years.

Almost all the buildings are preserved, and they reflect an impressive range of urban taste in the 1930s style. These buildings were not old when the waves of reconstruction began in the 1950s and, moreover, most were apartment blocks – that is, they comprised multiple private dwellings with multiple owners, a factor that made a building's purchase and demolition more difficult for developers.

I think of all these things as I wander around the city. Many foreigners – and even Greeks – divide the city into ancient and modern without a second thought. But just as ancient Athens is not a unitary city – it encompasses many historical periods, including its revival during the reign of the Emperor Hadrian (CE 117–138), the greatest Athens-lover of them all – so, too, the modern city lacks any single form. Moreover, that distinction leaves out the medieval city, not least the unique Byzantine

is approved, and Georgios Papadopoulos installs himself as president of the republic.

November 1973
Athens Polytechnic students protest against the regime. The occupation of the campus is bloodily repressed with the intervention of the army.

20 July 1974
Turkey occupies the northern part of Cyprus following the junta's attempt to overthrow the Makarios government on the island. The Colonels are forced to resign. Recalled from exile, Konstantinos Karamanlis (of the Nea Dimokratia/New Democracy party) forms a government of national unity and restores democracy.

1981
Greece joins the European Economic Community; in 2001 it also joins the European single currency.

2004
Athens hosts the twenty-eighth Olympic Games. The city gains new infrastructure, and existing facilities are upgraded.

2009
Newly elected prime minister George Papandreou (PASOK) reveals that the country's public accounts were manipulated by preceding governments in order to join the European Union.

'Athens constantly fires the imagination in so many ways; it exists almost as a mythological place, outside of history.'

chapels dating from the ninth to twelfth centuries; those that were saved from the town planning of the nineteenth century and from the excavations to bring the Ancient Agora back to the surface are important reminders of a time that is still in semi-obscurity. Athens has lost many traces of the 'interim' era, from Hadrian to the city of Otto and Amalia, the first royal couple of the new state. Also forgotten is the Frankish Tower on the Acropolis. It survives only as a hazy memory in old photographs taken prior to its demolition in 1874.

Older Athenians recall their childhood years in the 1930s, when the development of Athens really got going. The only shadow was the dark political spectre that loomed over the whole of Europe. Greece had been under a right-wing dictatorship since 1936 and a restored monarchy since 1935. Despite that, the Metaxas government was Anglophile, so it kept out of the Axis. The Occupation, as the Greeks call the period of the country's fascist and Nazi rule, was a grave interruption in the progress of the capital. The positive developments of the inter-war period were disrupted; there was famine in the city; the infrastructure was dismantled. The civil war that followed (1944–9) caused enormous destruction, with buildings blown up and many others left in a state of disrepair. By 1950 Athens was a city desperate to look to the future.

All of this hit my own generation like a shock wave. As a child I experienced the reconstruction taking place all around me.

2010
Greece's debt reaches 350 billion euros. The EU, the European Central Bank and the International Monetary Fund allocate the first bailout package: 110 billion over three years in exchange for severe austerity measures.

2012
The second bailout plan is approved in March. The most violent public disorder since the start of the crisis takes place.

2013
Unemployment hits 28 per cent. The government closes the state-owned broadcaster ERT.

2015
Austerity policies lead to a severe social crisis: GDP collapses by 25 per cent. Syriza, the left-wing party led by Alexis Tsipras, wins the election on a promise to renegotiate the bailout plan and end austerity but fails to win an absolute majority by two seats: it therefore forms an alliance with the centre-right party ANEL. The neo-Nazi Golden Dawn win seventeen seats. At the same time the migrant crisis also breaks out: in the space of a year, almost 900,000 migrants arrive in Greece by sea. (See also 'A Decade of Crisis' on page 58.)

2019
Kyriakos Mitsotakis of the New Democracy party becomes prime minister with an overall parliamentary majority.

Few have fought harder for the preservation of Greek artistic and cultural heritage than Melina Mercouri. As minister for culture between 1981 and 1989 she made the push for the return of the Parthenon Marbles from the British Museum one of her most memorable battles. And Melina Mercouri was not a woman one could easily ignore: an internationally renowned actress (the 1960 film *Never on Sunday*, for instance, won her Best Actress at the Cannes Film Festival), after the military junta's 1967 coup she became one of the most influential voices protesting against the dictatorship, leading to her exile and the revocation of her citizenship. After the regime's fall she returned to Greece in 1974 and became even more politically active: before becoming a minister she was a co-founder of PASOK, the centre-left party that won the 1981 elections. Mercouri believed that Greece should prosper thanks to its cultural heritage, and in her eight years in power she brought a ministry that had previously been marginalised into the centre of the political debate, promoting action and bringing an energy to the political scene. We owe the survival of many neoclassical buildings in Athens to Mercouri as well as the creation of an archaeological park in the Greek capital and the establishment of the European Capitals of Culture initiative in 1985, when Athens became the first to hold the title.

At the time it was not unusual to see both humble homes and grand mansions being torn down to make room for modern apartment blocks. Athens changed enormously and, year after year, its form began to disappear. Yet again, however, another political transition – the fall of the seven-year military junta in 1974 – opened up a new perspective on the city. On one hand, the demand for the modernisation of society took on a new urgency; on the other, an affection for the 'real' Athens took hold. In the 1970s a nostalgia for the city that was lost began to grow – a lost cause, to be sure, but not without some successes. Until that time very few buildings were protected by law. This began to change after 1975, and, from 1978, under Stefanos Manos and later Antonis Tritsis and Melina Mercouri at the Ministry of Culture, a systematic approach to the urban challenge started falling into place. It was in those years that hundreds of houses in Athens came to be protected by preservation orders.

Athens will change again. The economic crisis – a social and cultural cataclysm – has created an impatience for the new. As I observe the urban ruins I try to imagine their future. The Athens of 2030 will have new priorities, and, assuredly, at the top of the list will be a desire for the city to be synchronised with the new paths our century is paving. But what drives emotional attachment to any city is the hidden meaning of its history. Athens constantly fires the imagination in so many ways; it exists almost as a mythological place, outside of history. That is where I will return whenever I attempt to reconfigure the city that raised me. 🖎

Athens: tourists on the Areopagus.

THE PASSENGER   Nikos Vatopoulos

The Odeon of Herodes Atticus at the foot of the Acropolis.

Lands of Migration

In a sea of indifference and racism, there are still havens of welcome and hospitality. The Greek islands, chief among them Lesbos, have in recent years seen an influx of asylum seekers shut out by 'Fortress Europe'. Displaced people have passed through these lands since time immemorial – and their inhabitants have not forgotten their own roots.

MATTEO NUCCI
Translated by Alan Thawley

A temporary installation on the statue of the Mother of Asia Minor in Mytilene, Lesbos, during an international demonstration against the 2016 agreement between Turkey and the European Union that prevents thousands of migrants from leaving the island.

'I sing of arms and the man who of old from the coasts of Troy came, a refugee of fate, to Italy and the shore of Lavinium.' – Virgil

The most famous of the ancient refugees who took to the sea from the shores of Asia Minor was Aeneas.

We cannot say with any certainty from where he – along with his father, his son and dozens of survivors of the sack of Troy – set sail. Visiting the famous city, besieged by the Achaeans for ten years before it fell thanks to Odysseus' wooden horse, we struggle to see the sea on the horizon. Although its power had grown through trade – its position almost guarding the Dardanelles – Troy was never a maritime city. The land surrounding the defensive walls – which Heinrich Schliemann announced he had identified in 1872 – has certainly changed over the centuries. The Scamander – the river in which Achilles massacred the Trojans after taking up arms again to avenge Patroclus – is now just a trickle known to the Turks as the Karamenderes, a name with no legendary significance. Today, the plain where the warriors' bodies were buried is an expanse of fields that stretch anonymously towards the wine-dark sea; there is no invitation to visit, no signs, and the little roads that run across the landscape form a labyrinthine grid. When you arrive at the strip of sand, amid the fierce silence of the waves beating against the shore, it is hard to imagine that this was where the Achaean ships once anchored. Black tree trunks litter the beach among plastic refuse, bottles and scraps of clothing left by those who have taken to the sea. Strange metal constructions have been built by families seeking shade in summer. No one mentions the modern migrants.

Not far from the shore, or so it seems, is an island known as Bozcaada that now belongs to Turkey but which the Greeks have always called Tenedos. It gives the impression of being close enough to protect any boat that sets sail, but the reality is very different – if you are unprepared the sea will show no mercy. And yet you will have this same feeling, that of an enclosed and protective sea, everywhere along the coast of Asia Minor. Let's turn around the southern tip of the region known in antiquity as the Troad, beyond present-day Babakale. In Virgil's account, when Aeneas left the shores where he had grown up in a prosperous city with high hopes for the future, with an auspicious birthright (as the son of Aphrodite and a distant cousin of Hector, the ablest of King Priam's children), rather than setting out from the coast opposite Tenedos he left

MATTEO NUCCI is a Roman author who has studied ancient philosophy and published essays on Empedocles, Socrates and Plato, editing and translating the latter's *Symposium* for the Italian publisher Einaudi. His first novel, *Sono comuni le cose degli amici* (Ponte alle Grazie, 2009), was shortlisted for the Premio Strega, as was *È giusto obbedire alla notte* (Ponte alle Grazie, 2017). More recent works include his essay *L'abisso di Eros* (Ponte alle Grazie, 2018). His articles and travel reportages are published in the weekly supplement of *La Repubblica, Il Venerdi*.

from a town called Antandros, the port the Trojans used for their timber trade. Today, only a few stones remain of Antandros. Much more interesting is Assos, a few kilometres away, where Aristotle came to live for two years just after Plato's death in 347 BCE. There the great thinker occupied himself mainly with scientific research. He found a wife, made some good friends and met Theophrastus, who became a loyal collaborator, and he lived contentedly, not least because it was so easy to visit the island facing the town with his friends and colleagues. It is so close that on fine days you can see the coast so clearly it is as if you could reach out and touch it. Even then Lesbos was an island with a rich history. It was said that the head of Orpheus had washed up on its shores after he was killed by women driven to fury by his rejection of their advances. Orpheus, the legendary poet who almost succeeded in bringing his wife Eurydice back to life and who, after seeing her disappear for eternity into the dark of Hades, decided to devote himself exclusively to music. Perhaps it was the singing head of Orpheus that endowed Lesbos with the lyrical magic that achieved glory in the immortal poetry of Alcaeus and Sappho; and perhaps it was the lake-like calm of the sea that inspired the Trojans to venture out and abandon their homeland. Aeneas did not set sail for Lesbos, however, as people do today in large, unbelievably overcrowded rubber dinghies, united in their certainty that the Greek shore is but a stone's throw away. Aeneas eventually arrived in Rome; for modern migrants just reaching Europe would be enough. Crossing the imaginary border drawn in the sea just off the Turkish coast is the decisive step.

The majority of the thousands of asylum seekers who have arrived on Lesbos in the past few years have left Turkey from these same beaches. Between Antandros and Assos, evading the ever-tightening surveillance of the border forces, those who do not drown first land somewhere near Skala Sikamineas, a little village nestling in a magnificent fishing harbour. From the taverna, which is open year-round, even on the coldest days, and named after a local poet, it seems impossible to imagine shipwrecks in this flat expanse barely eleven kilometres across. 'You can drown a few metres from the shore,' an old fisherman bent over his nets tells me. 'All it takes is panic, some vicious rocks and little waves that can seem insurmountable when you're in the water. The sea is harsh everywhere, but on land things can sometimes be worse. Why risk so much if you're going to have to stop here?'

In these few sentences he had summed up the drama that has played out here in recent years. Drama is an ancient Greek word formed from the verb *drao*, which means to act. Drama is action. Because any action, any decision, brings suffering. Yet nothing creates more terrible suffering than being unable to act, and that is what has been happening on the islands off the Turkish coast since March 2016, when the highly contested agreement between the EU and Turkey decreed that the people who had risked death to get there would have to stay there.

I was in Idomeni at the time that may one day go down in history as the worst turn on the road towards the destruction of the European dream. Idomeni is a little village of 150 people on the northern border of the Greek province of Macedonia, eighty kilometres from Thessaloniki. Its position on the railway line, during the months when thousands of migrants were travelling the so-called Balkan route to northern Europe, was crucial. It even became famous in a way when some Balkan nations within the

'Walking around in the evenings between the fires outside the shelters was a moving experience. While a few kids had found friends to play with, the parents were preparing food, and the youngsters were gathered at the meeting points to charge their phones.'

EU gradually closed their borders (against EU regulations that forbid this happening between member states), forcing their diminutive neighbour, then known as the Former Yugoslav Republic of Macedonia (since 2019, following a long-running dispute with Greece, simply the Republic of North Macedonia), to follow suit and block the passage of those who had got to that point. A double chain-link fence was hastily erected along the border, and the police were armed with rifles loaded with rubber bullets and tear gas while thousands of refugees clustered around the now defunct railway tracks. According to official estimates, the settlement that grew up during those months became home to more than fifteen thousand human beings. For the most part Syrians fleeing a ruinous war, Afghans, Kurds and Iraqis, they found themselves trapped, forced to live in whatever tents they could muster, surrounded by mud. This was an absurd situation that would have become untenable without the assistance provided by NGOs and volunteers. Back then we had not yet understood that the enormity of what was happening would lead Europe, under German guidance, to seek an agreement with Turkey that would previously have been difficult to imagine. A complex deal that is still subject to challenges because it is not on the list of legally recognised international treaties. Above all, it is a deal with devastating consequences for the flow of migrants across the Greek sea because, as all observers know, it has created a sort of internal border within Greece that is entirely alien to any legal or rational norm, one that prevents people from leaving the islands off Asia Minor and moving freely through Europe, except in cases where the long process for recognition of refugee status reaches a positive conclusion. But in those days of the emergency in Idomeni, people had their minds on other things. Walking around in the evenings between the fires outside the shelters was a moving experience. While a few kids had found friends to play with,

A refugee, Lesbos.

NUMBER OF REFUGEES PER HEAD OF POPULATION

Ratio of first-time asylum applicants
to populations of EU countries (2018)

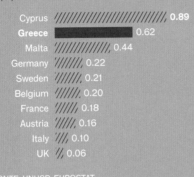

Cyprus	0.89
Greece	0.62
Malta	0.44
Germany	0.22
Sweden	0.21
Belgium	0.20
France	0.18
Austria	0.16
Italy	0.10
UK	0.06

FONTE: UNHCR, EUROSTAT

TOTAL NUMBER OF ASYLUM APPLICATIONS IN THE EU

Millions of first-time asylum applicants

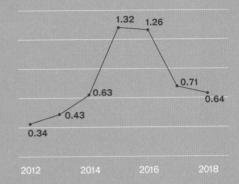

0.34 — 2012
0.43
0.63
1.32
1.26
0.71
0.64

2012   2014   2016   2018

LANDING POINTS OF REFUGEES

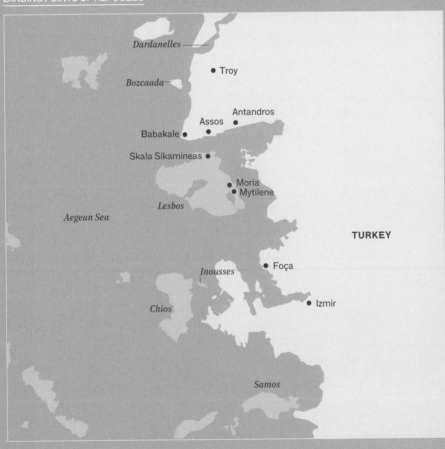

THE PASSENGER   Matteo Nucci

the parents were preparing food, and the youngsters were gathered at the meeting points to charge their phones. You would hear heartrending tales and possibly also horrific legends, such as that of the Greek doctor who had provided passage through the mountains for some unaccompanied young children but had allegedly then sold them on to organ traffickers. But there were also beautiful stories, and one of them rightly became celebrated. It was about an elderly local woman who opened the doors of her house every day to those in need, offering them a shower, a little rest, some peace and quiet. Just a drop in the ocean but one with extraordinary symbolic significance. Panagiota Vasileiadou, eighty-two years of age, told the journalists who gradually arrived to interview her that she herself was the daughter of refugees, and that she had personally felt the weight of tragedy, a tragedy that no Greek can claim to have forgotten even though it now appears distant and almost lost amid the many absurdities of the twentieth century.

It was 13 September 1922 when the final Catastrophe took place in Smyrna (modern Izmir). *Katastrophi*. This is still how people remember the end of the Greco-Turkish war, which also signalled the end of an entire civilisation. The coasts of Asia Minor had been home to Greek peoples since the Iron Age, the days of Aeneas, and even before Aeneas. Then, in 1919, almost a century after Greek independence from the Turks, who had dominated Hellenic territory since 1453, the Greeks tried to take

A dump in Lesbos piled with life-vests and boats used by migrants crossing from the Turkish coast.

THE GRECO-TURKISH WAR

In 1919 a Greek expeditionary force landed in Anatolia, claiming a need to protect the local Greek population from the Muslim Turks. In the Sèvres Treaty of 1920 Athens obtained Thrace and the Gallipoli peninsula along with Smyrna and its hinterland, bringing it closer to achieving the project known as the *Megali Idea* (the Great Idea), in other words the reacquisition of all the territories that had belonged to the Byzantine Empire and were still inhabited by the Greek diaspora. Mustafa Kemal, known as Atatürk, the 'father of the Turks', led the resistance movement that sought to reconquer the lost territories, and a violent conflict ensued. Although the Greek army achieved numerous victories in the initial phase, it capitulated in the face of Turkey's 'great offensive' of 1922 and was forced to beat a retreat. In September the districts of Smyrna inhabited by Greeks and Armenians were burned down. At least thirty thousand people died. The city of Smyrna, a symbol of peaceful cohabitation between Turks, Greeks and Armenians, was destroyed in what the Greeks still call the Catastrophe of Asia Minor. The Treaty of Lausanne, signed in 1923, annulled the previous Treaty of Sèvres and ordered an exchange of populations on the basis of religious identity. Over a million displaced people, many of whom did not speak Greek, swiftly arrived in Athens, which saw its population double, with major consequences for the urban landscape. The Catastrophe marked the end of the Great Idea and the Greek presence in Asia Minor.

back what they had never stopped regarding as theirs. The *Megali Idea*, the Great Idea, proposed a restoration of the territorial integrity of the Byzantine Empire and reconquering the Polis – as it is still called by Greeks – the city of Constantine, better known to us as Istanbul. The capital would have been moved from Athens to Constantinople, and many Turkish lands would have returned to Greek control. The great powers that Greece had sided with during the First World War did not offer the promised support, however. The words of Great Britain and France turned out to be empty, and Kemal Atatürk revealed himself to be an extremely astute strategist. In 1922 the Turkish counter-offensive vanquished the Greek contingents, which had almost reached Ankara, and the end of the Great Idea was sealed by the great fire of Smyrna, the elegant and cultured Greek city that is now the Turkish city of Izmir. One of the young reporters who described the atrocities of those tragic days would become perhaps the most influential American writer of the twentieth century: Ernest Hemingway. While the Greeks threw themselves into the water in an attempt to reach the ships and were pushed back by those who ought to have brought them to safety, the American was struck by what was at first sight an incidental detail, and it became the epilogue to one of his best-known short stories. In 'On the Quai at Smyrna' (first published in the 1930 edition of *In Our Time*) he depicts the fleeing Greeks breaking the forelegs of those pack animals they were unable to take with them and dumping them in the water, the whole scene being, in his words, 'a most pleasant business'.

Hemingway's minimalist irony is an attempt to avoid rhetoric in a situation where it could be employed by the tonne. The end of Greek civilisation on the shores of Asia Minor led to a monstrous migration. As well as those who fled the flames of Smyrna or Turkish persecution, thousands of families were involved in a dramatic exchange of populations in an attempt at pacification that remains unstable even today. The Greeks in Greece and the Turks in Turkey. But how can you define the culture of peoples who have been intermingled for so long? Religion was the key: Christians over here and Muslims over there. More than 1.5 million people abandoned everything and took to the sea, carrying with them what they could. Some stopped on the islands off the Turkish coast – Lesbos, Chios, Samos and Kos – but most migrated to Piraeus, the port of Athens, or maybe to the port of Thessaloniki. It was a disturbing exodus, a movement of people with profound consequences for twentieth-century Greece. And yet those displaced people who suffered terrible conditions and died of hunger and exhaustion in their thousands (around seventy thousand) were never denied the opportunity to leave, to seek elsewhere the future that had been taken away from them in Asia Minor. Never before on the islands off the coast of Asia Minor – in other words, in the original heart of the very idea of Europe – had a plan been hatched to stop the flow of migrants. Never. And perhaps this is why recently, outside the shacks and the tent cities, outside the improvised encampments and the cabins thrown up by NGOs, I so often saw Greek women and men hard at work lending a hand without show, without self-aggrandisement,

The Moria migrant camp, Lesbos.

without fuss. The old lady in Idomeni was not a unique case wheeled out for the press. And it was not only those who had experienced the migration of 1922 at first hand who offered their help. Wherever the migrants were stopped in their search for dignity – in the districts that had actually sprung up in Chios to accommodate people displaced from Smyrna, beside Vathy's cemetery on Samos, in the fields outside Mytilene on Lesbos – I always felt I could detect a bewildered look on the faces of people witnessing families who had left everything and were forced into inertia with no idea of how their future would take shape. And, along with this bewilderment, a human propensity that is absolutely unique in these days of growing obsession with national sovereignty, racism and the collapse of solidarity, something related to the word for foreigner, *xenos* – but, rather than the familiar term xenophobia, its exact opposite, *philoxenia*, friendship towards strangers.

This, too, is an ancient story. In Greece there are no stories that have completely lost their connection with the dimension from which they originated, because myths, stories and events have entered and shaped the DNA of the people. Perhaps we should go back to Odysseus, that other migrant, who was forced to roam the Mediterranean for ten years before he could reach home. There was a decisive moment during his adventures. The Homeric poets describe it entirely without grandiloquence, perhaps with the same literary and human intentions that inspired Hemingway almost three millennia later. It was the morning that Odysseus found himself shipwrecked on the island of the Phaeacians. After sleeping in the bushes, dirty and naked, the hero emerges on to a beach where some girls are playing with a ball. It is a wonderful, unexpected scene. Princess Nausicaa stays while her companions run away screaming. She talks to the stranger with composure and explains what he should do to be welcomed by her parents. Sure enough, following the girl's instructions Odysseus finds himself at Alcinous' table shortly afterwards without ever being asked his name, what he is doing, what he wants and where he is going. These were the key rules of the institution that the ancients simply knew as *xenia*. Because while *xenos* meant foreigner, above all it meant guest. And *xenia* was, very simply, the duty of hospitality to be shown to foreigners when they arrived with no bad intentions. You will see for yourself if you arrive as an ordinary traveller, unannounced, in a village in Greece or the regions of southern Italy known to the Romans as Magna Graecia because of their populations of Greek settlers. You are unlikely to want for company or not to meet someone who offers you a glass of water and invites you to pull up a chair outside their house, to rest in the

'If you arrive unannounced in a village in Greece or the regions of southern Italy known to the Romans as Magna Graecia you are unlikely to want for company or not to meet someone who offers you a glass of water and invites you to take a seat outside their house.'

shade in the summer or in the sunshine in winter, before you continue on your way.

This is what is happening on a very different scale to those who have come ashore in recent years, having fled war and barbarity. I remember a Syrian family on Lesbos, at the Moria camp, one of the most talked about migrant camps because in the past few years it has exceeded its maximum capacity almost fivefold. They were a husband and wife of about forty with two teenage children. The mother burst into tears while telling me about Aleppo and the drama of not being able to move on, the drama that would not be a *drama* from a strictly etymological point of view and for that very reason becomes intolerable. The husband was searching for wood to improve their shelter – I have no idea how. The children were outside in a wonderful community centre called One Happy Family, where a group of Swiss helpers had joined forces with Greeks to create areas for sport and recreation as well as holding language classes and running a medical and dental emergency service. As she fell back into silence, I asked her if she wanted to give me her telephone number. Perhaps I could be of some use to her. At that point she broke into a smile and gestured for me

An Afghan refugee, Lesbos.

not to worry. So many people had helped them, she told me. Many local Greeks had swapped numbers with them. They had actually been surprised, not imagining that the Greeks would be so accommodating. They really were good people. Poor, of course. A country where the two of them – professionals with children whose future was just opening up to them – would struggle for prospects. To go somewhere else, to move on, that was what the Syrian woman wanted, like most of the recent migrants, to head towards wealthy northern Europe. But that is the problem: they can no longer continue their journey.

Travelling around the islands neighbouring Turkey in recent years, looking for every parallel with mythology and history, the events that came to mind most often were those described in detail by Herodotus in his account of the first wave of migrants for which we have certain testimony. This is the story of Phocaea, one of the Greek cities that was besieged and occupied by the Persians in the sixth century BCE; one of the many Greek cities abandoned by its citizens when they fled across the Aegean to seek their fortune elsewhere. It all happened one night in 545 BCE. The walls surrounding Phocaea were tall and strong; it is said that the money to build these almost impregnable defences had come from King Arganthonios of Tartessus (roughly corresponding to present-day Andalusia), who had been very impressed by the spirit of the Phocaeans. They were an exceptional people: extraordinary sailors, great traders, full of curiosity, sublime doctors and also experts in deception and piracy. So when Harpagus, the commander of the Persian troops, went so far as to construct a hill outside those powerful walls so they could storm the city, the Phocaeans immediately understood their fate. They requested one night to consider the terms of the surrender but instead set sail in their swift ships across a dark sea, calm as a lake, to find their first refuge on Chios. If you ever have the opportunity, do visit these places described by the world's first historian. Phocaea is now known as Foça to the Turks. It still stands on a double bay as it did in Antiquity, and the remains of the city conquered by the Persians are ruins on the arid hill that stands behind the town. Fishing boats crowd every quay, and in the evenings the streets are filled with the smell of grilled fish and fried squid from the restaurants. But the important thing is the sea and that little stretch of water between the coast and the islands, even

more sheltered than that between Tenedos and Lesbos. Here, as well as Chios across the water, there are also the little Inousses Islands. The sea really does resemble a tranquil lake that any sailor would be capable of tackling – an option taken by inhabitants of all the ancient

cities besieged by the Persians during that period, the same that those fleeing Smyrna in 1922 thought they had.

On that night in 545 BCE, however, although the sea remained calm and benevolent, the outcome was contradictory. The people of Chios had no love for the Phocaeans. This is an important part of the story, because the tendency to idealise the past can undermine the lessons that can be learned from history. Despite their negative opinion – caused principally by the piratical cunning of the Phocaeans – the people of Chios offered the customary welcome reserved for anyone fleeing a war, an invasion or a famine: there were no exceptions to the laws of *xenia*. As was always the case, the newly arrived refugees were offered emergency assistance, then they were asked their intentions. The Phocaeans certainly had a plan: to settle on the Inousses Islands. Not far from home, in other words, with the same sea and the same climate. But the people of Chios objected. No pirates in the neighbourhood. Nowadays this makes us laugh – and not

THE PASSENGER   Matteo Nucci

just because the Inousses have for years now been the home of Greece's hugely wealthy shipowners, who are notorious for not paying their fair share of taxes, but because the Phocaeans' contribution to Mediterranean civilisation went far beyond piracy. Herodotus tells us the whole story. What is important is that there was no barrier, no closed camp, no impediment to the refugees' chances to create their own destiny. The Phocaeans set sail again and arrived in Corsica, remaining for five years in what is now Aléria. Disputes with their neighbours, the Carthaginians and the Etruscans, led to a bloody naval battle in around 540 BCE, which the Phocaeans won. Nevertheless they took again to the seas and soon found the place where they would settle once and for all. It was on the coast to the south of Paestum (in the modern Italian province of Salerno) where they caught sight of a double bay that reminded them of home. There was a spring nearby called Hyele, around which they built what would become the famed city of Elea, taking its name from the spring. It became an important centre of medicine, and among its first-born (those we would now call second-generation migrants) was Parmenides, who would go down in history as a philosopher, poet and doctor of body and soul. A thinker who indicated in his poem the one unchanging way of truth as opposed to the path of opinions in which human beings are so wont to lose themselves. Parmenides' path of truth passes through the gate of day and night, which can still be seen in the Porta Rosa of Velia – that is, Elea – one of the most interesting and lesser-known archaeological parks in Italy.

But European agreements on migrant movements take no account of history, philosophy, Parmenides or Herodotus. There is no new Elea on the horizon. Today's rallying cry is to defend ourselves, stop the flow and bar the way. According to official estimates, some eighty thousand migrants are now stuck in Greece; eighty thousand people of different ethnicities denied, for an unspecified length of time, the possibility of crossing the country's borders. Around a fifth of them are on the islands off the Turkish coast covered by a 'geographical restriction'. The Council of State was called upon to rule on this measure, even though its decision to annul it had little effect, since it was immediately circumvented by other provisions, as is the way of things in these days of apparent legality. The most attentive observers of the migrant phenomenon say there is a bigger plan behind the creation of defined areas into which migrants can be crammed, one developed in Australia: to present those who have decided to flee their homeland with a prospect so forbidding that it becomes preferable not to flee. This is the so-called 'No way' model, as the Australians, with short memories of their own history, have called their operation. The thousands of migrants intercepted on boats before they come to shore are transported, in spite of the high cost, to far-flung Pacific islands over which Australia exerts huge economic power (the best known being Nauru). Crammed into migrant camps run by a private police force that is not answerable for anything to anybody, in miserable conditions that very few people have had the opportunity to investigate, migrants are condemned to an infinite wait for a response to their

Sunset over Lesbos.

asylum requests. 'No way' conclusively became a template when it inspired Viktor Orbán, the first and most fanatical of the European champions of national sovereignty. Deporting migrants to camps built in a zone comparable to the Pacific islands was not an easy task, but evil has its own creativity. The idea of building an immense defensive structure of electrified chain-link fencing just inside the effective borders of Hungary enabled Orbán to create a 175-kilometre buffer zone. The camps in which the migrants are detained have been built in the zone, and there they are forced to live in undignified conditions while they await their turn to request asylum. An inhumane non-place where all rights are suspended, where there are no prospects and where people become a different class of human being. Thanks to the migrants' ability to communicate with those back home who have not yet left, this black hole can help to circulate the message: don't take to the seas if you are trying to flee, because, to paraphrase the 'No way' video slogan: if you

don't have a visa, whether you are a family, a child, an unaccompanied minor, it makes no difference; there is no hope for you.

The plan is failing in Greece, however. The islands refuse to become non-places. And, in spite of all the efforts to create horror, the Greeks continue to do everything to prevent horror from gaining the upper hand. You only need to visit Lesbos, the island that has become a symbol of the crisis. Where even the pope came to send out a message at that critical time when hundreds of people were arriving every day, and where the international press gathered for months and continue to do so every time the Moria camp offers the possibility of a scoop. Come any day of the year – better in winter when the warm sea, Mytilene's famous ouzo and the music of the tavernas cannot cloud your judgement. As soon as you arrive, amid the smoky bustle of the port, you will forget immediately about the naval ships anchored there ready to intercept the boats and dinghies on the maritime border. You'll be surprised how busy it is. Slip into a café. There are lots of them, but two in particular will suit your purpose: Bobiras and Π (the Greek letter pi). At any time of day you will find young people sitting and eating, chatting and smoking in an amazing ethnic melting pot. Young people from Greece and every corner of Europe who have come here to work, sitting down with their counterparts from Syria, Afghanistan, Congo and so on; some studying, others talking, laughing, arguing. Complete normality, in other words. A surprisingly cosmopolitan atmosphere on an island that until a few years ago was accustomed to almost exclusively Greek tourism plus a few Turkish holidaymakers who came to eat sardines washed down with ouzo, the odd Scandinavian, some French visitors and a few Italians. So are these two bars

'These have always been lands of migration. They have always offered a first haven for those fleeing Asia Minor. And so, ultimately, the *genius loci*, the spirit of the place itself, conspires against certain decisions and plans.'

I've mentioned unusual? I have asked many people on my wanderings around this magnificent island, from the beaches where Aristotle and Theophrastus catalogued five hundred species of animal to those where Sappho grew up, besieged in recent decades by women under the spell of the primordial god Eros. I have put the question to a thousand NGO workers in their nurseries, refectories and meeting places. In the bars and in the fields I have asked the peasants who work in the sun and in the rain. I've put it to people who live next to the Moria camp and who cannot bear for much longer the theft of their vegetables, fruit and animals but raise their eyebrows as if it were something inevitable. But none of them gave me as clear an answer as Patric, a young man who came here with the UNHCR without much enthusiasm but then fell in love with the island. He quit his job with the United Nations' refugee organisation and got one in internal security at the Moria camp. Patric explained to me that Lesbos, in spite of all the difficulties, had changed profoundly since 2015 – and for the better. Anyone who says the opposite is lying. There's an abstract reason: having been used to a low level of European tourism, the islanders are now living on a multi-cultural

island that is almost a model for the future. 'Contact between people brings huge benefits, but let's put that to one side,' he told me. Born in Sweden to a Lebanese father and a Swedish mother he says he is biased, and he is in danger of falling into the familiar rhetorical traps. 'The clearest and most indisputable aspect is the economic development. Jobs in every sector. New shops, bars and clubs of all kinds. Demand and supply. The famous rules we always go back to and forget as soon as they don't suit us any longer.'

But the best explanations of how this island has become an example of development, employment and culture are not enough. Was this not one of the geographical areas destined to become a non-place? Certainly it is difficult to imagine that the island touched by the spirit of Orpheus' music could be compared with Nauru or the cold, harsh fields of Hungary between the fences and the border. The same goes for Samos, the island of Hera and Pythagoras, or Chios, the island that, according to ancient tradition, was the birthplace of the blind poet Homer. These have always been lands of migration; they have always offered a first haven for those fleeing Asia Minor. And so the *genius loci*, the spirit of the place itself, conspires against certain decisions and plans. A representative of the European institutions offered an explanation. There is no way that Orbán's plan could succeed here. These people are Greeks, accustomed to 'forgetting' about one migrant here, helping another there,

An Afghan refugee, Lesbos.

'Today, on the Greek islands off the Turkish coast, lands that tell the story of migrations dating back thousands of years, we are seeing what is perhaps the most terrible catastrophe unfold. The catastrophe of those who believe they can defend the indefensible and stop the unstoppable.'

smoothing the path for one procedure, ensuring another one fails – essentially, all the burdensome, exasperating, convoluted Levantine bureaucracy for which Greece, with its reliance on personal connections and its deficiencies, disorganisation and its genuine ability to take you by surprise, is famous. It can kill off all hope sometimes, but it can also kill off the most destructive plans, and that is what matters now.

Off the coast of Asia Minor we are seeing one of the most perfect demonstrations of an ancient concept that we think we have absorbed, although we have actually lost sight of its real significance. We are seeing with our own eyes the deep meaning of the word crisis, which we have been repeating for years like idiots. What is a crisis? *Krisis* in Ancient Greek means a choice or decision. *Krinein*, the verb from which the noun derives, means to separate, divide or choose, so a crisis is the moment when you need to make a choice. Because we are at a crossroads, will we go one way or the other? The writers of ancient tragedies constantly presented this aspect of a crisis. In their worldview they gave us a warning: any choice brings pain; whichever path we take we are destined to suffer. But no path will ever be worse than lack of action, the inertia of those who stop at the crossroads and refuse to choose to avoid the pain.

In these years of crisis, the idea of defending ourselves, of building a fortress by the crossroads and putting up walls and fences to protect what has already been swept away by history, is eating away at the men and women condemned not to choose with an even more putrid form of misery. Frustration, rage, anguish, desire for revenge, acrimony, rancour, these are the overwhelming feelings among those who are stuck, unable to move, full of hatred for everything that threatens the world they had become accustomed to, unable to see that destruction lies in immobility and having obstinately decided that we must not move from the crossroads. By denying themselves the opportunity to act and therefore falling into the worst form of drama, the kind without a future, those advocating defence to the bitter end imagined that they could also stop those who, faced with their own crossroads, did take that huge decision. Today, on the Greek islands off the Turkish coast – which some would like to turn into non-places, not realising the impossibility of such an undertaking in these lands that tell the stories of migrations dating back thousands of years – we are seeing what is perhaps the most terrible, and in some senses grotesque, catastrophe unfold. The catastrophe of those who believe they can defend the indefensible and stop the unstoppable. No rhetoric could ever describe a situation like this. Perhaps we have only disdain – or the irony dripping with anguish that brought Hemingway's story of the tragedy of Smyrna to a close: 'My word, yes, a most pleasant business.'

The Lost Generation

The Greek crisis is becoming, above all, a demographic crisis. Hundreds of thousands of young people have left the country and now feel remote and resentful, an attitude shared by those who were unable to leave and so find themselves doubly frustrated. A dejected generation who have been deprived of their future.

CHRISTOS IKONOMOU
Translated by Konstantine Matsoukas

The Athens Metro.

'One feels greater sorrow for what one has had and lost than for what one never had.' It is 2,500 years since Pericles, the man who allied his name more than any other to one of the most hallowed periods of ancient Greek history, addressed this phrase to the Athenian citizens mourning the first casualties of the Peloponnesian War. This is a phrase whose import is universal and timeless (as are many of the phrases in Pericles' 'Funeral Oration' passed down to us by Thucydides) because it encapsulates, with breath-taking clarity, the deep bond that links the feeling of loss with the function of memory and consciousness. We feel pain about loss because we *remember* what we have lost, because we *feel nostalgic* for what we have lost. We feel pain about the things we have lost because we are aware that, along with them, part of us is lost, too. And it is precisely this indissoluble bond between loss and memory that impels one of the heroes in my book *Good Will Come from the Sea* to wonder: 'We lost our jobs, our homes, our lives – why can't we lose our memory, too? Why? Why did they take everything else but leave us our memory? Why couldn't they take that, too, while they were at it?'

Loss, memory, consciousness. These forces have the leading role in the fictional universe I strive to create. They are forces at work in the human condition generally and particularly in the multi-faceted crisis that has been plaguing Greece over the past decade. They are forces directly related to one of the most telling consequences of the crisis – the massive exodus of thousands of young Greek men and women, abandoning their homes to seek a better future either abroad or elsewhere in Greece. This is a whole 'lost generation', as it has been called – although, as often happens in such cases, the characterisation only conveys part of the truth and of reality. There are many issues hiding behind the analyses, the numbers and the statistics. And it is those issues that I endeavour to address in my books. As far as I am concerned, literature is not just a mirror of reality but mainly a mirror of things invisible. Quality literature is perhaps the only art form able to speak so incisively and vitally about the unseen or hidden aspects of our existence at both a collective and an individual level. And, for me, that is precisely where the ethos of literature rests: in its ability to bring us face to face not merely with the unknown or invisible aspects of our existence but also those aspects that we do not wish to face because they are not appealing, because they are repellent, because they smudge our polished reflection, the burnished image we have of ourselves.

*

The crisis in Greece started showing its teeth after 2009. It is estimated that since then at least 400,000 people have left the country, not just for countries in northern and western Europe but also for Australia, the United States, Canada – the rich nations of the Gulf, too. This is a phenomenon with critical implications if we consider certain basic facts:

- First, the majority of these people are young, educated and highly specialised.

CHRISTOS IKONOMOU was born in Athens and has published four collections of short stories, two of which have been translated into English: *Something Will Happen, You'll See* (Archipelago, 2016) and *Good Will Come from the Sea* (Archipelago, 2019). *Something Will Happen, You'll See* won Greece's Best Short Story Collection State Award in 2011. His books have been translated into seven languages.

> 'It seems that Greece has not only lost its present but its future, if we reflect that these people are the generation whose task it is (or ought to be) to find a concrete expression for the new vision of Greece.'

- Second, most of them were driven away by the crisis because they deemed that Greece could not offer them prospects for a better future.
- Third, they do not, by and large, intend to come back to Greece, at least not in the foreseeable future.

In other words, it seems that Greece has not only lost its present but its future, if we reflect that these people are the generation whose task it is (or ought to be) to find a concrete expression for the new vision of Greece: a country with a creative, productive economy and a just, functional state.

The situation becomes even more complicated as there are many young Greeks who want to leave the country but fear they do not possess the educational and vocational qualifications necessary in competitive job markets abroad. Many of these chose the path of internal migration, abandoning the large urban centres ravaged by the crisis – such as Athens, Piraeus and Thessaloniki – and opting either for smaller cities and villages on the mainland or for the islands of the Aegean and the Ionian Sea, aiming to set up new lives there. Most look for job opportunities in the fields of tourism (traditional and alternative), farming, commerce and small enterprises. People such as these are the lead characters in *Good Will Come from the Sea*, including the anonymous narrator quoted near the beginning of this article, who wants to overcome the ravages of memory (a futile hope, indeed!) because he knows full well that one feels greater grief for what one has had and lost than for what one never had.

*

Every migration is a tragedy and every migrant is a tragic person. I do not use these terms in the current sensationalist way. Tragedy is the conflict of truth with truth. In the face of the migrant (whether s/he realises it or not) two of the greatest truths of human nature come into conflict: the need for faith and the consequences brought about by loss of faith. It takes faith to distance oneself from one's language, people, country, history, culture. It takes faith to get over the doubts, trepidations and fears that justifiably arise in the wake of deciding (or being forced) to settle in another country, looking for better living conditions, a greater chance of safety, more opportunities. Are all those things there to be found, or will these expectations fall flat? Will they be able to adjust to the new environment? And what might happen if they realise they are not welcome in the new country?

Migration, then, is an act of faith and simultaneously an act resulting from the loss of faith: the migrants have lost faith in their homeland. They have stopped believing that the homeland can provide the things they need. Loss of faith creates a deep wound in the soul. And although that wound can heal, its causes are hard to forget.

The new Greek migrants bear that wound in their souls, consciously or unconsciously, to varying degrees.

Margarita, fifty-two, moved from Thessaloniki and now offers farm stays up a hill in the little town of Plomari, Lesbos.

Fed up with city life, Tallidis, forty-eight, moved from Thessaloniki and opened a small workshop in Mytilene, Lesbos, where he sells his jewellery.

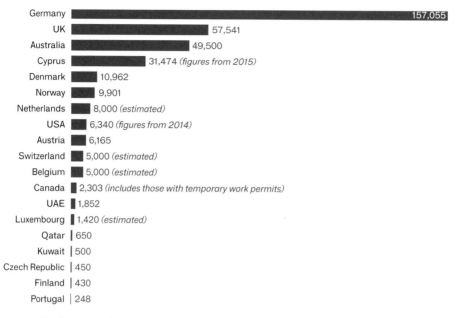

Germany	157,055
UK	57,541
Australia	49,500
Cyprus	31,474 *(figures from 2015)*
Denmark	10,962
Norway	9,901
Netherlands	8,000 *(estimated)*
USA	6,340 *(figures from 2014)*
Austria	6,165
Switzerland	5,000 *(estimated)*
Belgium	5,000 *(estimated)*
Canada	2,303 *(includes those with temporary work permits)*
UAE	1,852
Luxembourg	1,420 *(estimated)*
Qatar	650
Kuwait	500
Czech Republic	450
Finland	430
Portugal	248

Total: 354,791 *(not including figures from France, Sweden, Italy and others)*

A DECADE OF CRISIS

In 2009, in the midst of the debt crisis, the socialist government led by prime minister George Papandreou (PASOK) embarked on a revision of the public deficit, which had been undervalued by previous governments up until the country joined the eurozone. The deficit/GDP ratio was 15 per cent – compared with the 3 per cent allowed under the Maastricht Treaty. The markets were in chaos, and Greece was insolvent. In May 2010 the eurozone and the International Monetary Fund approved a first bailout package, worth 110 billion euros, in exchange for a drastic programme of austerity: 30 billion euros of cuts in three years. The debt continued to rise, unemployment soared and the country slipped ever deeper into recession. In early 2012 a second bailout package was approved (worth 130 billion euros), with an agreement that included a 53 per cent devaluation for investors in Greek bonds. With the country under the control of the troika (the European Commission, European Central Bank and International Monetary Fund), the government had no financial room for manoeuvre and was unable to bring an end to the recession. A debate began on a Greek exit from the eurozone, dubbed 'Grexit'. Europe presented Alexis Tsipras (elected in early 2015) with a new programme of aid in exchange for new and painful reforms. In July Tsipras asked the Greek people to reject this austerity plan via a referendum. He negotiated and obtained a new plan (86 billion euros in loans) before resigning and being re-elected in September 2015. In 2017 Greece's debt stood at 178 per cent of GDP (repayments of the bailout packages and international loans are to be spread over thirty years), but the country was slowly returning to growth.

This trauma connects them to the older generations of migrants who left the country en masse at the beginning of the twentieth century and later, in the first decades after the Second World War. There is, however, a big difference between then and now – one that relates to Pericles' dictum above: the old migrants never knew a Greece better than the one they left behind; today's, however, have known (or think they have known) a better Greece than the one they are forced to leave behind. To put it another way, it is one thing to leave behind a poor country and something completely different to leave a country that you can remember when it was not impoverished.

And there is another, even greater difference. The old migrants were convinced that the Greece they were leaving could not offer them a better life. Modern-day migrants are convinced that the Greece they are leaving does not *want* to offer them a better life. This is a Greece that punishes the worthy, the honest, the hard working and rewards the dishonest, the truants and those who manage to climb the vocational, social and economic ladder by devious means, exploiting the opportunities offered by party allegiances, nepotism and political patronage. To be sure, I do not claim that the response to the ills that plague the Greek state is always a sincere one. I know very well that some of those who rail against the system do so not because they truly believe it is warped but because they are, quite simply, not part of the system themselves. Nevertheless, there are just as many young Greeks who feel like foreigners in their own country. And those among them who do not wish (or are unable) to leave it, are prey to a feeling of entrapment that, in turn, exacerbates uncertainty, insecurity and fear. And fear, as is well known, is the breeding ground of hate: you hate yourself for being afraid; you hate all the things that make you fearful; you hate those who are doing nothing for you to stop being afraid. From that point on it's a small step to the position of Rita, the young internal migrant in *Good Will Come from the Sea*. Narrating to a friend her tragicomic adventures in trying to find a job, she confesses, with chilling clarity, her deeper wish: 'You know what I want more than anything? I want this whole country to disappear off the map. To shrink to a tiny tiny tiny speck and then to fucking vanish off the map, to just cease to exist. That's what I want, that's it. For this whore of a country to disappear off the map for ever.'

*

The lost generation of the Greek crisis: an army of young people who are leaving, have left and will continue to leave their homes in search of a better life either abroad or in the country's interior; people who walk in the shadows, carrying in their minds and hearts the darkness of despair and the light of hope. Their path from dark to light has a tragic aspect to it, although that is often none other than the element of tragic irony. It is a telling fact of the contradictions and confusion that define modern Greece that many of the Greeks who left the country once the crisis broke out settled in Germany, the country which, according to the majority of their compatriots, is more responsible than any other for the ills plaguing Greece today. Equally ironic is the fact that several of the new Greek migrants express anti-European sentiments while at the same time capitalising on the advantages and opportunities offered

Kostas moved from Thessaloniki and opened a pizzeria in Mytilene, Lesbos, a year ago.

Nikoletta, thirty-two, decided to leave Athens for Mytilene, Lesbos, where her family has its roots. Six months ago she moved to the island with her husband and two-year-old son Orfeas.

'It is a telling fact of the contradictions and confusion that define modern Greece that many who left settled in Germany, the country which, according to the majority of their compatriots, is more responsible than any other for the ills plaguing Greece today.'

them, by virtue of being EU citizens, to improve their living, educational or vocational standards in other countries of the European Union. Yet the greatest irony is that many of the new Greek migrants seem to have discovered everything that's wrong about Greece only once they had to leave Greece. And now, having settled in other places, they look at their country from afar with their vision blurred by vengefulness and speak of it with words that drip poison. 'Greece should operate as a tourist resort,' one of them told me a while ago. 'It should be open for business from May to October and closed for the rest of the year.'

The worst thing, though, is not that there are so many young migrants who express such negative feelings about their homeland – where they saw sunlight for the first time, where they uttered their first words, where they played their first game, where their heart first skipped a beat through love or longing or fear. One might say they managed to escape what they considered a prison. But what about those who didn't have the same opportunities? What about those who continue to live in Greece not because they choose to but because they cannot escape from that prison? How to live while feeling like a stranger in your own homeland – feeling like an exile, a convict, an outcast in your own country? How can people live in a

country that they are poisoning and which is poisoning them?

The lost generation is not just the young leaving because they can no longer remain in Greece, it is also those who are staying in Greece because they cannot leave.

*

It is not my intention either to glorify or to make tragic heroes of the lost generation – besides, most of them do not see themselves as tragic or heroic. The matter of modern-day Greek migration (internal and external) concerns me – as a Greek, as a European and, mainly, as someone trying to create literature – because, in my opinion, it is a parable about the moral crisis afflicting not just Greece and Europe but the West as a whole.

Despite its severity and its sweeping consequences, the political, economic and social crisis in Greece is not accompanied, as far as I can tell, by a moral crisis, a crisis in consciousness. I don't see around me many people able (or, at any rate, willing) to wonder if we, as a society, really are who we want to be, who we think we are, who we declare ourselves to be. I don't see many people around me wondering, honestly and soberly, if there might not be a great gap between our way of existence and the values and ideas that we (supposedly) espouse and defend. I don't see many people around me willing to put to the test – in deed not in word – some at least of the convenient lies, widespread myths and conventional perceptions that we have cultivated about ourselves and our relationship with others. And I don't see many people willing to admit that, finally, values, principles and ideas, no matter how noble and refined, take on real meaning only when we fight to internalise them and make them part of our own consciousness, only when we fight to make them binding for our own existence. Alternatively, they are nothing more than slogans. Good slogans, noble slogans, apt slogans, timely slogans – but still just slogans.

This moral crisis (or, rather, its absence) derives from the fact that most of us refuse to accept that we all have a degree of responsibility for what is happening around us. We are collectively responsible for the fact that (to paraphrase Tolstoy, who, let it be said in passing, believed that the only revolution possible is a moral revolution) we all want Greece to change, but none of us wants to change ourselves.

We keep on looking for new messiahs, refusing to question whether the problem is not the old messiahs but, rather, our very need for messiahs. Our need, that is, always to transfer the responsibility for change to some 'enlightened' leader, of the left, the right, the centre-left or the centre-right. We disguise our own indifference, our own inertia, our own apathy, our own unwillingness, in the indifference, ineptitude, apathy, unwillingness we see in each particular messiah. And we do this because we are looking for a convenient and useful alibi for our own inertia, because it is convenient and useful to nurture the illusion that everything is someone else's fault. And, despite the continuous refutations, despite the fact that today's and yesterday's messiahs have failed

During the crisis years, amid severe concerns over debt, some people have ridden the wave of desperation and loss of trust in the system, championing surreal theories as a complete escape from reality. Artemis Sorras entered the fray in 2012 with a promise to pay off the country's debt using his '145 trillion-euro fortune'. Put simply, he was going to sort the situation out, and, being a generous man, he was going to repay not just the country's debt but also the private debts of all of Greece's taxpayers. Mr Sorras, whose 2014 income declaration in fact amounted to no more than 20,000 euros a year, claimed that much of his fortune derived from his shares in the defunct Banque d'Orient – a bank that was closed down in 1936. (You can actually still buy these shares, but only as collectors' items on eBay.) Along with his nose for finance, Sorras also declared he had discovered an ancient aerospace technology and a new type of fuel that would easily take us to Mars. In 2015, on the basis of these and other outlandish ideas, he established the Convention of Greeks, a political movement that before long had opened over two hundred offices and signed up thousands of supporters, convincing them to pay twenty euros for a membership card, plus a monthly subscription that would allegedly enable them all to write a goodbye letter to the state and the Greek banks: I will no longer be paying, as *he* will settle my debts. There was only one possible ending: Sorras's arrest for money laundering, fraud and criminal conspiracy, accompanied by demonstrations of solidarity from many of his devoted followers.

In an Athens bar with Yianni.

THE PASSENGER   Christos Ikonomou

to meet our expectations, we continue down the same path. Why? Because, in my opinion, we never do feel let down by our leaders. We never feel let down because, in truth, we do not believe what our leaders tell us and we do not believe what we say among ourselves. We say we believe in the values of meritocracy, transparency, equality before the law, social justice, legitimacy – but we need to at long last ask ourselves if we have, in fact, internalised all these values, if we truthfully consider them binding for each of us individually. I mention this because I have the impression, not to say certainty, that most of us want everything to change in Greece on the condition that such changes – which, of course, are difficult and painful – do not concern us but everyone else. I also have the impression, not to say the certainty, that most of us want everything to change for everyone – except for us.

I fear that we continue not to understand – or pretend not to understand – that a country such as Greece with so many serious intrinsic problems will never be able to stand on its own feet and prosper thanks only to its leaders' efforts, no matter how honest, competent or consistent those may be. Naturally, I share the view that leaders – that is, political leaderships – have primary responsibility insofar as they possess power. I share the view that not all leaders or all those in government or all politicians are the same – although I have good reason to suspect that power is everywhere and always the same. But I also share T.S. Eliot's view that the actions and behaviour of the rulers are determined by the collective ethos of the ruled. Hence, if we truly want to change Greece we might start by trying to change something in the small Greece each carries inside of us and the small Greece that surrounds each one of us. And, if we want to change the world, we might want to start with the small world each of us carries inside and the small world that surrounds each one of us.

I am not optimistic, but I am hopeful. I am hopeful because I always have in mind what Chekhov said: 'There is nothing good that didn't come out of some sewer.' Consequently, yes, maybe the Greece of the crisis is a bottomless sewer, but, out of that sewer good will come. Out of that sewer good *has to* come. I am hopeful because I believe that a writer's highest achievement is hope. But it is the hardest thing to attain because, as St Paul says, visible hope is no hope. What we hope for cannot be made visible because this would do away with the need for faith. Hope is not something that exists in its own right, not an abstract concept, not something to be found outside of us, far from us. Hope is not a pre-election slogan, an advertising strategy or a motto in a self-help manual. Hope is a creation. Our creation. We build hope with all the things we do or don't do. Hope is maybe our strongest weapon against the fear of death. Hope is the resistance to the oppression of the human spirit and of human existence, by the fear of death. As far as I am concerned, then, writers are called to do just this: to provide, through their work, a platform to hope rather than to the fear of death. To provide a platform to life, not death. ✒

Once Upon a Time: The Greek Taverna

Petros Markaris, culinary enthusiast and creator of the series of detective novels featuring Inspector Haritos of the Athens police, explains how eating habits have changed in Greece over the past few decades. In Athens, the legendary taverna, with its simple dishes and Mediterranean flavours, is growing increasingly rare as it gives way to new Greek fusion food.

PETROS MARKARIS
Translated by Konstantine Matsoukas

A traditional Greek taverna.

Greece is in an earthquake zone, and Greeks often use the term 'arc' to refer to a high-risk seismic area, such as those of Athens or Corinthia, but also more generally to any alignment of things.

Besides the arc of Piraeus Street, which transformed a former industrial area into a Via Appia of culture and the arts, there is, in the same district, a second arc, which we might call the 'entertainment arc' or the 'arc of fun'. This begins at Constantinople Street, just above the point where it intersects with Iera Odos. One of its branches runs into Petrou Ralli Street, while the other turns left into Iera Odos, meets Piraeus Street, continues through the Gazi district up to Persephone Street and there enters the districts of Thissio and Petralona. What I am calling the entertainment arc is a huge area full of bars, restaurants and nightclubs, and Iera Odos and Piraeus Street become virtually impassable on Saturday nights. Coming out of Gazi on to Persephone Street, and extending as far as Constantinople Street, you'll find a selection of eateries that cater for all tastes and budgets.

As soon as Athenians have had their fill of improving their minds with artistic and cultural activities they'll be on the hunt for gastronomic and alcoholic pleasures of the flesh. Questionable behaviour, perhaps, but easy enough to explain. In Greece meals are taken in the late afternoon and then later in the evening. Theatres and cinemas don't open at seven o'clock but at nine, and dinner is always taken after a show – which explains why, in Athens, you can still find a hot meal even as late as 2 a.m. in some restaurants. It's a nightmare for me when I'm in Germany or Switzerland, where – with the exception of Berlin – restaurant kitchens close at 10 p.m. and the only place to get anything to eat is the railway station or an Italian restaurant. In Athens you can go to the central meat market on Athinas Street and dine at 6 a.m. when the trucks arrive and the drivers sit down in the market's two restaurants to get their strength up with a bowl of soup.

Tastes in Athens have changed radically in recent decades. Since the 1960s there has been a gradual disappearance of the traditional courtyarded tavern and the old-fashioned kitchen that sometimes opened only at noon and other times in the evening, too. In the 1970s it was still possible, in central areas such as Gyzi, to find establishments that were food shops

PETROS MARKARIS was born in Istanbul to an Armenian father and a Greek mother and speaks and writes Greek, Turkish and German. He has worked with Theo Angelopoulos on various screenplays, including *Eternity and a Day*, which won him the Palme d'Or in Cannes in 1998, but owes his international fame to his novels featuring Inspector Costas Haritos. The first four books in this series have been published in English: *Deadline in Athens* (Grove, 2005), *The Late-Night News* (Vintage, 2005), *She Committed Suicide* (Arcadia, 2009) and *Zone Defence* (Vintage, 2011).

'Today retsina consumption is half what it was in the 1970s and its quality exceptionally low. In this, a decisive role was played by the gradual disappearance of the taverna and the wine bar.'

during the day and operated as tavernas at night, making use of the stock the owner held – olives, feta, mackerel and sardines – and complemented by the cooking of the shopkeeper's wife.

In Athens and throughout the country there were traditionally three types of eating place. First, the tavernas, places exclusively for night-time meals, occasionally with music – even if the entertainment was initially restricted to a couple of guitars and a singer, as in the interwar years (the orchestra came to the taverna much later). The second was the *oinomageireion*, a wine-bar-cum-kitchen that offered a limited selection of cooked dishes served with wine – and by wine I mean retsina. The third was the *zythestiatorion*, a restaurant that also stocked beer. These were not like British pubs or German *Bierkeller*; these hostelries served food but with more choice on the menu and beer on sale – beer not being a common drink in Greece at the time. Only a few restaurants and coffee houses served it. Greeks, and Athenians in particular, drank only retsina and only from the barrel. There was no taverna or wine bar in Athens that didn't offer retsina from the barrel – and rightly so, because retsina is a sensitive kind of wine that cannot be bottled or transported. It was drunk only locally and only from the wood. Retsina's decline began during the junta (1967–74) when one company started bottling it commercially. At the end of the 1970s the price of wine was deregulated – up to that time it had been controlled. Prices started to rise, and grape growers preferred to sell their produce for expensive wines, whereas retsina was a cheap wine for popular consumption. So the lowest-grade grapes ended up being used for retsina, and the quality plummeted. Today retsina consumption is half what it was in the 1970s and its quality exceptionally low. In this, however, a decisive role was also played by the gradual disappearance of the taverna and the wine bar.

Then, came the 'meat era', when tavernas began to reinvent themselves as grill houses. It took the Greek middle class about twenty years from the end of the Civil War in 1949 to discover the joys of going out to eat meat, a social activity that remains popular today.

The latest development is relatively recent, dating roughly from the early 1990s, and goes under the generic term 'new Greek cuisine'. It is a style of dining – which flourishes particularly among the upper middle class, intellectuals and artists – the paramount feature of which is the elimination of every traditional Greek taste. Apart from the Italian influence in the Ionian Islands, the cuisine that has prevailed throughout Greece since 1922 has been that of the migrants from Asia Minor – a bourgeois version of the noble cuisine of Smyrna and Asia Minor. It is the food with which generations of Greeks have grown up and which, in Greece, had evolved over time into a more Mediterranean style, with vegetable dishes cooked in olive oil (*ladera*) being served alongside versions of Turkish dips and sauces such as tzatziki, which in Greece is thick like cream, whereas in

THE ELECTRIC

Line 1 of the Athens Metro, known as
the *Ilektrikos* (the 'Electric'), connects
the Kifissia neighbourhood in the
north with Piraeus. It was built in
1869 and initially linked the centre of
Athens on the slopes of the Acropolis
– with around 50,000 inhabitants –
to Piraeus, a city that was home to
10,000 souls at the time. The idea
for a railway line running through the
whole of the city dated back to 1835, a
year after Athens had been named the
capital of the Kingdom of Greece. In
1904 the line was electrified, earning
it the nickname still used to this day,
even though it is now just one of the
lines of the Athens underground.
The characteristic wooden carriages
in use until the 1960s have been
replaced by metal seats, while most
of the stations were renovated for the
2004 Olympics. Only five examples
of its nineteenth-century splendour
remain: Piraeus, Kifissia, Monastiraki,
Omonia and Viktoria. The article by
Petros Markaris published here is
taken from his book *Quer durch Athen*
('Across Athens'), which looks at the
different neighbourhoods of Athens
taking the Electric's twenty-four stops
as its starting point and offering a
glimpse of the city and its inhabitants.

Turkey it is thinner and eaten with a spoon.
Or that long-suffering dish moussaka, the
Greek take on which is completely different
from its Turkish cousin. New Greek cuisine
is an indefinable blend of meats, exotic
fruits and vegetables and sauces made with
avocado, coconut milk, crabapples and the
like. The big down side of this new Greek
cuisine is that it has taken the traditional
Mediterranean flavours out of the food
of Greece.

Somewhere between the grill house
and new Greek cuisine, the tastes of the
taverna and the wine bar – offering a
selection of simple dishes, for the most
part prepared on the day – disappeared
pretty much everywhere. The first blow
came with souvlaki; the final assault with
the spread of fast-food outlets. Both are
part of the empire of grill houses. More
and more often I find myself passing by
fast-food joints where I see couples in their
sixties – that is to say, people who grew up
with the taverna and the wine bar – sitting
with plastic trays in front of them eating
hamburgers.

Petralona is the only area of Athens
where you can still find tavernas with
traditional cooking. Everywhere else, at
least in the centre of the city, they are
tucked away in hidden spots and side-
streets where you only come across them
by chance or seek them out because you're
local and you know about them. One still

READY TO EAT

In Greece, 'ready to eat' or cooked food (*magirefta fagita*) refers to dishes that are stewed or baked in the oven. They are prepared in the morning and then kept warm and served as soon as they are ordered. This marks them out from 'to order' (*tis oras*) dishes, which are mainly cooked on the grill.

survives in Kypseli, the area in which I live, yet in the 1970s there were around ten.

Petralona is comprised of two separate neighbourhoods that share the same name: Kato (Lower) Petralona and Ano (Upper) Petralona. The dividing line is the railway. To the right of Petralona station as you come from central Athens is Kato Petralona and to the left is Ano Petralona.

Kato Petralona is essentially a continuation of the suburb of Tavros, past Chamosternas Street. It stretches to Piraeus Street and has two very distinct sides. One is very much like Tavros – a working-class neighbourhood with the same houses, same streets, same collective fate in store for the people living there. But next to this another, more youthful Kato Petralona has been showing its face in recent years, and this falls within the entertainment arc. At present these two are at odds, but the outcome is predetermined. The mature face is doomed, for one simple and not at all happy reason: Kato Petralona, like Tavros, Moschato and Neo Faliro, has high levels of unemployment, especially among the young. Yet in all these districts, rather than jobs, cafés and bars keep popping up. It's as if someone has decided that fighting the boredom of unemployment is more important than actually getting a job. And this phenomenon is not restricted to these neighbourhoods. Many of the younger customers lounging about in the innumerable cafés in the centre of Athens are also contributing to the youth-unemployment statistics. The family that can't get them a job gives them some money to kill time with a frappé or a freddo cappuccino.

Ano Petralona is completely different. The distinction between *kato* and *ano* is very common in large cities such as Athens and Thessaloniki. A neighbourhood starts small and grows over time until it passes a

The interior of a traditional taverna in the Metaxourgio district of Athens.

ANTIPAROCHI

The real driver of Greece's post-war economic boom was the construction industry, which brought a sea of concrete to Greek cities, characterised by a typically Greek phenomenon known as *antiparochi*. This is a sort of deal between a construction company and the owner of a plot of land, which is exchanged for a four-room apartment or a pair of two-room apartments depending on its size and value. Starting in the 1950s, a massive exodus from the countryside contributed to whole suburban districts springing up in areas where land prices were very low. These were filled with estates of large apartment blocks, often built with low-quality materials to cut costs further. In the chapter of his book *Quer durch Athen* ('Across Athens') about the Moschato neighbourhood, Markaris writes: 'If Rome is the eternal city and Paris the city of light, Athens is the city of *antiparochi*.'

THE PASSENGER   Petros Markaris

Left: A traditional taverna
in the Metaxourgio district
of Athens.

Below: Thymios
in his taverna.

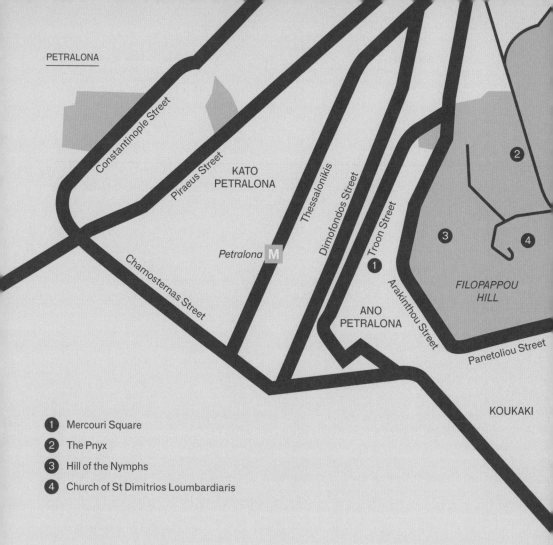

KATO
PETRALONA

Petralona M

ANO
PETRALONA

FILOPAPPOU
HILL

KOUKAKI

Constantinople Street

Piraeus Street

Chamosternas Street

Thessalonikis

Dimofondos Street

Troon Street

Arakinthou Street

Panetoliou Street

1 Mercouri Square

2 The Pnyx

3 Hill of the Nymphs

4 Church of St Dimitrios Loumbardiaris

GREEK FRAPPÉ

Walking through the streets of Greece at any hour of the day it is almost impossible not to come across someone drinking a frothy liquid known as a frappé through a straw. While in some parts of the world, the term refers to a milkshake, a frappé in Greece is a sort of iced coffee. It was created in 1957 when Dimitris Vakondios, finding himself without a kettle, decided to use a blender to mix his Nescafé with cold water, and since then it has become a sort of national drink. The frappé is made with instant coffee, water, sugar and milk and ice to taste. First the coffee and sugar are mixed with a small amount of water to form the foam, and then more water, milk (either fresh or condensed) and ice are added, and the whole lot is blended. Frappé can be drunk in three ways: *metrios*, with equal measures of coffee and sugar, *glykos*, with double the amount of sugar, and *sketos*, without sugar.

'The transformation in a people's attitude, way of life and tastes is encapsulated by the fact that the simple, ordinary food with which so many generations grew up has been turned into exotic fare found in only a few establishments.'

given boundary – a square, say, or a notable building – and then this extension starts being designated as *ano*: Ano Petralona, Ano Nea Smyrni, Ano Kypseli and so on. Usually *ano* indicates that it is a newer area, one more remote from the centre of the district, generally of a lower standard. Yet this isn't the case with Ano Petralona. On one side it borders Koukaki via Mercouri Square and, on the other, the foothills of Filopappou, and it is without question the more appealing of the two Petralonas.

If Kato Petralona is the extension of Tavros, Ano Petralona is the extension of Thissio, an exclusive nineteenth-century neighbourhood. Just as you pass from Tavros to Kato Petralona without noticing, so you move from Ano Petralona to Thissio. Kato Petralona is flat; by contrast, Ano Petralona is built on land that rises up towards the foothills of Filopappou with one- and two-storey residences that have survived the extensive reconstruction and the spread of apartment blocks.

The affinity with Thissio is also apparent in the fact that in Ano Petralona one still finds neoclassical buildings, as on Dimofondos Street, the main thoroughfare in the district. Evidently, these were built because Thissio expanded beyond its borders or because affordable land in Thissio became more difficult to find while property prices in Petralona were more attractive to prospective owners.

Although I have not counted them personally, I am sure that Ano Petralona is the area of Athens with the most acacias. One comes across them in Kato Petralona and Tavros, too, but their presence there is not so apparent. As you go down the streets at the foot of Filopappou – such as Panetoliou Street or Arakinthou Street towards Troon Street or Dimofondos Street – all the thoroughfares are lined with these trees.

The entertainment arc of Piraeus Street comes to a halt at the railway lines. The wining and dining changes radically in Ano Petralona. The bars are small and quiet, more for talking and less for listening to loud music. Here, one also finds the traditional tavernas and kitchens of Athens, such as Ikonomou, which still serves the classic dishes. A bit further on and you can sit in Pericles and His Wife and try the fried cod with skordalia, a traditional garlic dip.

The transformation in a people's attitude, way of life and tastes is encapsulated by the fact that the simple, everyday food with which so many generations grew up has been turned into exotic fare found in only a few establishments.

A few hundred metres down the road, where Dimofondos Street intersects with Poulopoulou Street, we enter busy, cosmopolitan Thissio.

The Apostate

In his two terms as mayor, Yiannis Boutaris balanced the books in Greece's second city, Thessaloniki, while promoting its Jewish and Ottoman identity to attract Israeli and Turkish tourists – and in the process enraging nationalists and Orthodox Christians.

JAMES ANGELOS

Yiannis Boutaris,
the former mayor
of Thessaloniki.

One night in the year 982, according to Orthodox Christian tradition, the archangel Gabriel descended from heaven for an earthly visit. Disguised as a monk, the angel arrived on Mount Athos, a secluded mountain peninsula dotted with Byzantium's most revered monasteries, to partake in a pre-dawn vigil before an icon of Mary and Jesus. 'It is truly meet to bless thee, O Theotokos, thou the ever-blessed and most pure, and the Mother of our God,' the archangel chanted with such celestial melody that a monk beside him understood he was in the presence of a heavenly being. The archangel then vanished, and for a time, according to some tellings, the icon emitted a divine light.

On a hot October Saturday in 2012 the same icon was delivered from Mount Athos to the shore of the northern city of Thessaloniki, Greece's second largest metropolis, aboard a Greek navy gunboat. The occasion was the coming hundredth anniversary of the city's liberation from the Ottoman Empire, and the monks of Mount Athos, a few hours' boat ride away, had seen fit to enhance the festivities by contributing one of their most venerated icons for a residence in the city. There on the paved harbourside to receive the icon were a military marching band, scores of Greek soldiers in navy whites and army fatigues and various politicians. I stood sweating among a crowd of a few thousand Greek citizens who had gathered around the city's most prominent landmark, the cylindrical, turreted Lefkos Pyrgos, or White Tower, built to fortify Thessaloniki during Ottoman rule. After an Ottoman surrender during the First Balkan War, the city came under Greek control in the autumn of 1912, on a day that seemed fated, as it fell on the feast day of the city's patron saint, Demetrios, a Roman military commander martyred there for his Christian faith in the early fourth century.

On an elevated stage sat the nation's highest-ranking clergy, all clad in black hats and cassocks. Flanking the clerics were two scruffy men dressed like Greek revolutionary brigands or *Tsoliades*, with pleated kilts and pom-pom shoes. They wore tired expressions, as if they had been rented out for such festivities one too many times. Offshore, a few clerics emerged from the cabin of the gunboat, their cassocks fluttering violently in the wind, followed by a pack of sailors carrying the icon, which was enclosed in a large case. The sailors loaded the icon on to a smaller coastguard boat that bobbed alongside the navy vessel, and then the priests, the sailors and their holy cargo puttered towards the harbourside. The crowd waited in silent anticipation as the faint, windswept din of

JAMES ANGELOS is a journalist who divides his time between New York and Berlin, writes for *The New York Times Magazine* and has contributed to publications including the *London Review of Books*, *The New Republic* and *World Policy Journal*. He is also the author of *The Full Catastrophe: Travels Among the New Greek Ruins* (Crown [USA] and Head of Zeus [UK], 2015) on the Greek debt crisis.

techno music echoed from the cafés lining the harbour, where young people carried on with their Saturday, apathetic to the sacred undertaking.

The icon was taken before the stage on which Greece's high clergy had gathered, and the clerics began to chant, uttering the same modal song of praise to Mary that the archangel Gabriel had sung one millennium and some decades earlier. The prayers and chants, however, were interrupted by a commotion.

'Accursed in front of us! Traitor!' Two monks lunged towards the then mayor of Thessaloniki, Yiannis Boutaris, a chain-smoking, tattooed, silver-haired man of scant size and seventy years. 'Boutaris, you degenerate!' one of the monks cried as they tried to set upon the mayor. A group of army officers intervened, grabbing the monks. Then police officers arrived and began dragging them away, tearing one of their cassocks in the struggle. 'You lust after Turks!' one of the monks cried.

*

I had first met Yiannis Boutaris about a year before at the Ritz-Carlton hotel in Istanbul, where he had been invited to speak at a local academic conference on Turkish–Greek relations. We met on the hotel's rooftop terrace late the night he arrived. The mayor was a sharp dresser with a fondness for braces and red socks while also possessing some of the qualities of an aged rock star. He spoke with a low, hoarse drone and seemed a bit dazed. Deep lines in his face suggested many years of partying. He smoked unfiltered Camel cigarettes almost continuously, as if his life depended on it. A blue-green lizard was tattooed below the thumb of his right hand, its tail running to the wrist – a reminder, he told me, of the reptile's capacity to regenerate after injury. In addition

EIGHT YEARS AS MAYOR

November 2010
Boutaris is elected mayor
(in office from January 2011).

October 2012
Boutaris is named World's Best
Mayor by the London-based
City Mayors Foundation.

August 2013
The Atatürk Museum is reopened
after three years of restoration.

May 2014
Boutaris is re-elected mayor
with 58 per cent of the votes.

January 2018
The construction of the Holocaust
Museum of Greece begins.

May 2018
Boutaris is assaulted by a group
of ultra-nationalists at an event
commemorating the Pontic Greeks
killed in the Turkish genocide.

November 2018
Boutaris announces he does not
want to stand again; he gives
his achievements as mayor a
rating of seven out of ten.

August 2019
The end of his second term
and retirement from office.

"'Thessaloniki was a booming city in the Ottoman Empire," Boutaris said. "It was a Jewish city and a Turkish city.'"

to his other tattoos, the symbol for his astrological sign, Gemini, appeared on the middle and ring fingers of the same hand. The gold stud in his left ear, he told me, protected him from the evil eye.

Boutaris had spent most of his life as a winemaker. He had inherited the family winery, which was founded by his grandfather in a mountain village just west of Thessaloniki in 1879. Since that time the region has been known for the sour black grapes that produce a dry red wine called Xinomavro. Boutaris is a recovering alcoholic who, for the past two decades, has tasted but not swallowed his own vintage. The family business – the Boutari Winery – at one point defaulted, and he used a considerable amount of his personal fortune to keep the company afloat, a financial hit from which he has never fully recovered. He eventually left the company solely to his brother and started his own smaller winery. The Boutari Winery, having rebounded from those earlier financial troubles, today remains one of Greece's most widely known wine brands.

Boutaris was in the company of an aide in a suit, Antonis Kamaras, a towering former banker who was educated at the London School of Economics and saw it as his job to soften the mayor's often blunt declarations into cohesive policy statements. Kamaras's father, a successful tobacco merchant, was a friend of Boutaris, and together the merchant's son and the mayor emitted an air of old aristocracy and somewhat faded wealth.

We found a table next to a three-piece band playing an assortment of Latin-flavoured New Age music. Boutaris lit a cigarette and crossed his legs. At one point a woman wearing a short blue skirt and stiletto heels walked by. Boutaris's head swivelled as his gaze followed her progress. He made a pained expression and then looked at Kamaras as if perhaps the aide could explain: how can such beauty exist? Kamaras, moving on as gracefully as he could, began to detail the mayor's efforts to draw tourists from Israel and Turkey to Thessaloniki by highlighting the city's Ottoman past. Boutaris then chimed in, 'Thessaloniki was a booming city in the Ottoman Empire,' he said. 'It was a Jewish city and a Turkish city.'

One may take these comments as simple fact considering that, at the time Greek soldiers wrested control of Thessaloniki from the Ottoman Empire, there were more Jews and Turks in the city than Greeks. But to refer to Thessaloniki – originally founded three centuries before the birth of Christ and named after Alexander the Great's half-sister – as anything other than a Greek city is to the mayor's detractors a provocation bordering on blasphemy. Yet, until the city became part of an expanding Greece, Jews composed its largest religious community and referred to it in Ladino (Judaeo-Spanish) as *la madre de Israel*, a bit of information Greeks were never taught in history classes at school. As Boutaris put it, 'They didn't know because nobody told them.'

Thessaloniki's Sephardim began arriving at the end of the fifteenth century after being forced out of Spain following the establishment of the Inquisition. They

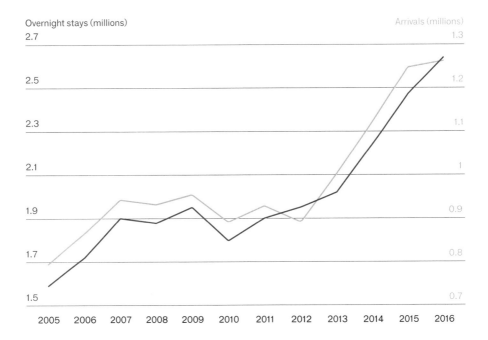

—— Overnight stays   —— Arrival

Overnight stays (millions)   Arrivals (millions)

SOURCE: THESSALONIKI TOURISM ORGANISATION

were welcomed by Ottoman authorities interested in repopulating the once thriving Byzantine city, whose Greek population had been decimated by the invading Ottomans decades earlier as punishment for resistance. Under Ottoman rule Thessaloniki became one of the largest Jewish population centres in the world, and Ladino was heard in the bustling port more often than Greek or Turkish. When the city became part of Greece, its Jewish residents were unsure about the change, fearful their liberties would be curtailed in a new nation that defined itself as Orthodox Christian. The Greek state nevertheless allowed Thessaloniki's Jews a large degree of self-governance. Jewish schoolchildren learned Greek and swore allegiance to their new nation.

But a profound metamorphosis was under way, one that precipitated a stark change in the makeup of the city.

Thessaloniki began to overflow with the Greek refugees who had been thrown out of their homeland, the budding Turkish state. The changes were accelerated by a massive fire in 1917 that destroyed much of the city, particularly the Jewish quarter. Many Jews left after this disaster, but around fifty thousand still remained in the city when the Nazis occupied it during the Second World War. The first deportations to Auschwitz-Birkenau began in March 1943, and, within a few months of cruel efficiency, Jewish life in the city was almost completely obliterated. Fewer than two thousand of the city's Jews survived. The near disappearance of Jewish life in Thessaloniki made it easier for residents of the city to ignore the fact that it had ever existed in the first place.

One month after taking office, however, Boutaris travelled to Israel. 'Not for nothing was it called the Jerusalem of the Balkans,' he said of his city in an interview with the *Jerusalem Post*, 'and it could be that again.' The mayor also told the newspaper that his first girlfriend was Jewish. During the same visit he spoke to a group of Holocaust survivors originally from Thessaloniki and asked them to help their city of origin by encouraging people to visit. These efforts seemed to pay off. In the first nine months after he took office visits to Thessaloniki from Israel quadrupled. Visits from Turkey also increased, although not so dramatically. The mayor was working on it, though. Thessaloniki, he told me at the Ritz-Carlton, is a must-see for many Turks, since it was the birthplace of Mustafa Kemal Atatürk, the founder of modern Turkey. Sure, Greeks blame Atatürk for the massacre and expulsion of Greeks living in Asia Minor around the time of the birth of the Turkish Republic in 1923, but 'whatever you think of him', Boutaris told me, 'he's a child of Thessaloniki'. Kamaras, the aide, interjected, making the point that this was a particularly controversial outlook for their city's residents, many of whose ancestors were those Greek refugees kicked out of their villages in Asia Minor. 'If you ask me, he is too outspoken,' Kamaras said. The aide preferred to put the mayor's views in terms of smart crisis-era economic policy. 'In light of the collapse of domestic demand, what we are trying to do is import demand from outside,' said Kamaras. 'Openness pays.'

The next morning I watched Boutaris give one interview after another to Turkish journalists on the hotel's terrace. The Turkish public – from leftists hostile to nationalism to Turkish nationalists pleased with Boutaris's apparent sympathy – exhibited great interest in the mayor, and it struck me that he was perhaps more popular in Turkey than in Greece. During the first interview that morning, Boutaris rolled up his sleeve to reveal a tattoo on his arm dedicated to his deceased ex-wife. 'Our life together was like a fantasy,' he told the journalist.

The journalist then asked him if he'd be willing to name a street in Thessaloniki after Atatürk. Earlier in his life Boutaris had suggested that the small street where Atatürk was born be named after the leader as a gesture to improve relations with Turkey. The idea was met with a fierce backlash in Greece. Rumours swirled that Boutaris wanted to rename

'In the first nine months after Boutaris took office visits to Thessaloniki from Israel quadrupled.'

THE PASSENGER James Angelos

the thoroughfare of St Demetrios after the Turkish leader. Boutaris abandoned the idea by the time he ran for mayor, although many Greeks still revile him for it.

'This is a delicate issue,' Boutaris told the journalist. The original idea was a gesture of 'moving forward' beyond the historical enmities, he added, but it had not gone over well in Greece.

'Can I say you hope to do it?' the journalist said. Boutaris squirmed a bit and seemed tempted to answer yes in order not to disappoint her.

Kamaras then saved his boss. 'The reaction to this suggestion was so strong we thought there were better ways to improve the relationship with Turkey,' he said.

In each interview that morning Boutaris repeated certain themes: Greece and Turkey have a 'very, very common heritage', the Greek mentality is similar to the Turkish mentality and he felt far closer to the Turks than to Europeans like, for example, Swedes. He mentioned repeatedly that Turkish Airlines offered direct flights to Thessaloniki from Istanbul and that visitors shopping in Thessaloniki 'won't believe their eyes at all the beautiful things they can find'.

One television journalist asked Boutaris if he thought the centenary celebrations would stoke animosities with Turkey. On the contrary, the mayor replied. It was a chance to highlight the commonalities between Greece and Turkey. The mayor pointed out that the Ottomans conceded the city to the Greeks without a shot being fired and that the first elected mayor of the city after its liberation was Turkish. 'I do not believe we have to celebrate the win,' the mayor said. 'It was not a win. It was a change of situations.'

Hearing this – a comment wholly out of step with the usual Greek national narrative – I wondered how he had ever been

THESSALONIKI'S JEWISH COMMUNITY

Over the course of its history Thessaloniki has welcomed Jews from many countries, notably those escaping the Spanish *Reconquista*, and for centuries it was a majority Jewish city. There were thirty-three synagogues with names that referred to the origins of their congregations, governed by the Talmud Torah Hagadol, an institution of seven representatives elected annually that was founded in 1520 and was linked to a school that trained rabbis for half of Europe. Thessaloniki was exceptional because, unlike almost anywhere else, the Jewish community was integrated with the other communities and was spread across the whole of society; when the city came under Greek control in 1912, 70,000 of its 150,000 inhabitants were Jewish and cohabited peacefully with Greeks, Turks and Bulgarians. The fire of 1917, which hit the Jewish community harder than others, marked a turning point: sixteen synagogues were destroyed, and many people had to move from the city centre, which was then predominantly inhabited by Greeks. Policies became less conciliatory, and anti-Semitic movements sprang up. The German occupation of Thessaloniki in 1941 marked the point of no return. During the Second World War 98 per cent of the Jewish community was sent to the extermination camps, and a census in 1951 counted just 1,783 survivors. One of the consequences of the genocide was the disappearance of Ladino, which had been the language of Greece's Jews for over five centuries: Shoah survivors discouraged their children from speaking Ladino, and as few as twelve people in Thessaloniki speak the language today.

elected mayor in 2010. His election win seemed to suggest that, in a time of deepening economic trouble, many Greeks were craving a new kind of politics. Boutaris, who was supported by a coalition of left-leaning and centrist parties, fused the pro-business tendencies more common on the political right with an aversion to the right's staid, nationalist inclinations. This was a rather unique combination in Greece, and people seemed willing to try it. Of course, it didn't take much to be considered a radical improvement over the previous mayor, a man named Vasilis Papageorgopoulos. Papageorgopoulos, a former dentist and sprinter who had won a bronze medal for his country in European competition and was nicknamed 'the Flying Doctor', governed the city as a member of the conservative New Democracy party for a decade. After Boutaris took office, his deputy mayor of finance – the first Jewish elected official in the city since the end of the Second World War – found that the city was deeply in the red and that the previous administration had apparently falsified the books. Two years later Papageorgopoulos and two of his aides were convicted of embezzling around €18 million and sentenced to life in prison. Papageorgopoulos maintained his innocence and appealed his conviction; the sentence was eventually reduced to twelve years.

Boutaris, in contrast, was able to balance the municipal budget within a few years of taking office. He intrigued the international press with his self-proclaimed reformist agenda and many tattoos. Journalists, looking for something good to say about Greece at a time when all the news was bad, heaped praise on him. *The New York Times* profiled him with the headline 'Greek Mayor Aims to Show Athens How It's Done', the UK's *Daily Telegraph*

with 'Greece's Vision of Hope', Germany's *Süddeutsche Zeitung* with 'A City's Last Hope'. At home, however, the feeling was more ambivalent. Much of his electorate clearly still despised him, particularly religious conservatives, as the outburst at the Panagia's welcoming ceremony had shown.

*

While the monks were berating the mayor, the bishop of Thessaloniki, a short man with a long beard, had a peculiar look on his face. He peered sideways in the direction of the commotion, resting both hands on his staff, his gaze not fully committed to the source of the disturbance, as it seemed to fall below the dignity of a bishop's full attention. It was hard to discern the expression behind the eyeglasses and grey hair that covered much of his face, but I wondered if perhaps what I was noticing was a look of pleasure.

Bishop Anthimos of Thessaloniki did not approve of Boutaris's talk about aspects of the city's past that did not fit its 'Helleno-Christian' identity. Such talk, as he once put it, resulted in the 'adulteration of our history'. The bishop often warned in his sermons of a panoply of supposed threats: territorial threats from the Turks; the threat coming from the country to the north of Greece that wished to call itself Macedonia (and is now named the Republic of North Macedonia), thereby appropriating Greece's Macedonian cultural inheritance; the threat of allowing gay pride parades in the city; the threat of European Union hegemony; the threat posed by immigrants; the threat posed by Islam; the threat posed by Jews. One Sunday from his pulpit the bishop warned about Jewish businessmen intending to buy property alongside Thessaloniki's harbour in order to build hotels and about a planned academic conference highlighting the city's

Yiannis Boutaris during a meeting of the municipal council while he was mayor of Thessaloniki.

Jewish history. The responsible authorities must clarify, he said, 'what exactly is going on'. He then came to his conclusion: 'The Jews are flirting with Thessaloniki.'

After the icon of the Panagia was welcomed by Anthimos and other clergy at the harbour, it was placed on a wagon hitched to the back of a camouflaged jeep for a procession to the Church of St Demetrios, where the bishop performs his sermons. The icon was led by the marching band, officers in full dress whites and soldiers doing a poor job of marching in step. Hundreds more solemn priests and monks trailed behind, and silent, darkly shrouded nuns carried lit candles, the wax dripping on to their hands. The procession passed the graffiti-tagged campus of Aristotle University, one of the nation's most well-regarded schools, where slogans like 'Never again fascism' and 'Victory to the struggle of the student walk-out' were sprayed on the shabby buildings. The campus is built on the site where hundreds of thousands of graves once constituted one of Europe's largest Jewish cemeteries. The cemetery was destroyed during the Nazi occupation at the bidding of Greek authorities eager to free up the land for the expansion of the university.

Once the icon arrived at the church it was carried past the green marble columns of the entrance and inside the sanctuary, underneath the high, open timber roof. A long line of pilgrims queued under the dim arcade and out the doors into the sunlight, waiting for what would be hours for a chance to make the sign of the cross before the icon and kiss the glass case covering it.

The Macedonian question began in 1991 when Athens opposed recognition of the Republic of Macedonia, which had been established following the break-up of Yugoslavia. The Greeks did not accept the Skopje government's choice of name, seeing it as a first step towards future territorial claims on the Greek province of Macedonia, which is the country's second-most populous and includes the city of Thessaloniki. Along with the dispute over the name was another that centred on the figure of Alexander the Great, whom both populations claim as a national hero. Athens's position prevented Macedonia from joining the European Union and NATO. In 1993 it became a member of the UN under the name of the Former Yugoslav Republic of Macedonia or FYROM. Tensions increased in 1994 when the Papandreou government in Greece placed an embargo on its neighbour. The embargo was revoked the following year after the European Community's protest at the European Court of Justice. The situation finally seemed to have been resolved on 12 June 2018 in a meeting between Alexis Tsipras, prime minister of Greece, and his Macedonian counterpart Zoran Zaev at Lake Prespa, one of the natural borders between the two nations. At the meeting, the governments of Athens and Skopje finally reached an agreement that should consign the Macedonian question to history, choosing the Republic of North Macedonia as the official name. The decision was not very popular in Greece, however, and sparked a new wave of protests across the country.

> '*Scattered throughout the city as they were, the Jewish headstones made accidental memorials, providing unmistakable reminders of the city's nearly blotted-out past.*'

The next morning I returned to the church as a doleful chant of 'hallelujah' came out over the loudspeakers perched on the façade. The line of worshippers waiting for a chance to kiss the icon had not diminished. Inside, I found Devin Naar, a young American historian from the University of Washington in Seattle with a particular interest in Thessaloniki and its Jewish past. I had met Naar, a lanky man with long, curly hair, a few days earlier at a Friday-night Shabbat service at Yad Lezicaron Synagogue, where the more religious of the thousand or so Jews who now live in Thessaloniki go to worship. Naar's ancestors were Sephardic Jews who settled in Thessaloniki in the early sixteenth century, and they founded a synagogue called New Lisbon. Centuries later Naar's great-grandfather took his family to America. Naar's interest in the city began with an effort to learn more about the grim fate of those family members who were still living in Thessaloniki when the Nazis arrived.

Naar and I passed the queue of those waiting to kiss the icon and descended a steep set of marble stairs into the crypt, where Roman-era ruins remain. We walked past a marble fountain and illuminated column capitals. Naar didn't pay much attention to the ancient displays. His eyes were directed towards the marble floor, where he was looking for headstones from the destroyed Jewish cemetery. After the cemetery's destruction the headstones were frequently used in construction projects and could still be found scattered around the city. In fact, one suburban home I saw was enclosed by a wall of Jewish tombstones, the Hebrew script and dates of death according to the Jewish calendar plainly visible. The Church of St Demetrios had been almost entirely destroyed in the massive 1917 fire and was rebuilt after the Second World War, when the headstones were in ample supply. Naar told me they were almost certainly used in the church's reconstruction. He photographed a slab of marble where he thought it looked like the Hebrew script had been chiselled out. We then walked to the yard beside the church where marble slabs were stacked in the tall grass. Most of them had old Greek writing on them, but some were tombstones with Hebrew script. As the sound of chanting clerics floated in the warm breeze, Naar walked through the grass examining headstones, looking, for a moment, like he might be overcome with emotion. He later pointed out that the preponderance of desecrated headstones had one unintended consequence: scattered throughout the city as they were, the headstones made accidental memorials, providing unmistakable reminders of the city's nearly blotted-out past.

*

A monolithic, ossified brand of Greek nationalism that has long concealed evidence of past pluralism has served to denigrate the concept of Hellenism itself, making it trite, insular and fragile. When coupled with the economic crisis, its logic also proved to have grave ramifications. Belief in Hellenic purity manifested itself in the rise of the fascist Golden Dawn, a

THE PASSENGER   James Angelos

The commemorative monument at Thessaloniki's old Jewish cemetery, which was destroyed during the Nazi occupation; the campus of Aristotle University now stands on the site. The monument was restored in 2019 after being targeted by several acts of vandalism.

party steeped in anti-Semitic, anti-Turkish hate. At the same time, in Thessaloniki, signs of a new openness were also evident. The city's residents, after witnessing the global attention and spike in tourist visits Boutaris had brought, appeared to see the benefit of embracing a more expansive view of their history. In the spring of 2014 Boutaris was re-elected with 58 per cent of the vote, a sizeable improvement on his previous victory margin.

Still, many of his detractors continued to loathe him and his vision for the city. Months after his second election victory Boutaris spoke at the unveiling of a monument at Aristotle University that memorialised the Jewish cemetery that had been there before. Standing beside the memorial – a collection of marble plaques alongside a broken menorah – Boutaris said his city had taken far too long to break its silence about its Jewish history. Since then, vandals have repeatedly defaced the memorial, at one point painting a large blue cross on it. In January 2019 the marble plaques were smashed to pieces. 'Even if they vandalise the monuments one hundred times, we will repair them one hundred and ten times,' said Boutaris. At the same time Boutaris was subjected to increasingly brazen threats and harassment. In May 2018 he was attacked by a nationalist mob in broad daylight. The mayor, seventy-five at the time, was punched, kicked and knocked to the ground. Afterwards, he called the attackers 'organised fascists' and vowed not to be intimidated.

Later that year Boutaris announced that, after two terms, he'd had enough of politics and would not seek a third. Which direction Thessaloniki would now take – towards nationalist mythology or towards openness and truth – remained uncertain. Boutaris, however, assured his supporters that the changes his administration had made would live on. 'It's a river that will continue to flow,' he said. 🖋

This article is an adapted excerpt from James Angelos's book *The Full Catastrophe*, published by Crown in the USA and Head of Zeus in the UK.

Kostas Koutsourelis

Kostas Koutsourelis paints a tragicomic portrait of the daily battle of Greek against Greek, amid suspicion of strangers, devotion to personal connections and unwavering solidarity in the face of the common enemy: the oppressive state.

Athenian Microdramas

Translated by Konstantine Matsoukas

Summertime, Athens, twenty metres below ground. Ambelokipi station at rush hour. A woman, seriously out of breath and loaded down with shopping bags, is fighting to find room in a packed carriage. The struggle is unequal, the crowd in front of her is dense and unwilling to let her through. The woman is sweating as she tries to balance acrobatically on the threshold, suspended between the train and the platform. Using her shoulders, her back, her hips, gathering her voluminous belongings tightly around her, she applies pressure to the inert mass of flesh behind her in an attempt to secure the few vital centimetres that will allow her to remain in the carriage. In vain. The passengers' repositioning, the redistribution of those few square metres immediately inside the doors, finally turns out to be too ambitious. The woman abandons her efforts. Loaded with her shopping, tongue lolling, she goes in search of another point of entry in a different carriage with fewer people.

Yet a mere few centimetres to the left and right of the standing space, down in the aisles in front of the seats, in the gangway connecting the carriages, it is not particularly crowded. With a simple one-metre step, a slight shimmy of the huddled chorus inwards, there would be enough space for the latecomers, even those bearing loads. Nevertheless, no one makes this shift. Those positioned by the doors especially would be ready to be crushed to death rather than sacrifice their proximity to the exit.

The inner recesses of the carriage appear to be an undesirable location. In the face of the newcomers, the 'old guard' give an orchestrated response: they dig their heels in and put out their chests as if to say, 'Actually, no. I'm *not* moving!' *¡No pasarán!* Those further back pretend not to be looking, pretend that the battle

KOSTAS KOUTSOURELIS is a poet and essayist born in Athens. He studied law and translation theory in Greece and Germany and has written poetry, essays and opera libretti. He has translated the work of Novalis, Octavio Paz, William Shakespeare, Rainer Maria Rilke and Gottfried Benn. His latest publications include a 2013 essay on Constantine Cavafy and the 2015 poem 'Gramma ston Odyssea Elyti' ('Letter to Odysseas Elytis').

being waged further forward is none of their concern. But they, too, are conveying a message to the frontiersmen: you hold on to your place, do not yield, don't think you will regain the space you conceded to others at our expense.

*

The entrance of an administrative building. A queue. The shape formed by the gathered crowd resembles a funnel more than it does a line: narrow at the stem, wide at the mouth. People stream in from every direction. There is no question of an ordered priority in the funnel. Rather, it's all a matter of flow, and everyone aspires to become the lucky drop that will manage to pass through the stem as quickly as they can.

The seventy-year-old woman (peroxide hair, tan leather trench coat, rainbow-coloured scarf, fabulously fashionable bag) strategically placed on the side to the left and back, places her dainty foot level with the shoulder of the guy in front of her. Surreptitiously, tentatively at first. In a short time, once she has ascertained he has zero intention of resisting, she bypasses him and moves in front of him. In like manner the entire family follows in her wake (45-year-old son, daughter-in-law and pubescent offspring).

A quarter of an hour later the family continues to advance as one, having gained at least three metres, always sneakily, inching up to and outflanking those ahead in the queue, one after the other. Behind them you can see others following their example, like a current in stagnant waters.

*

Greeks in public spaces are contradictory. It's hard for the foreign visitor to work it out. With visitors Greeks wear their Sunday-best smile; they are genial, affable, helpful. Between themselves, on the other hand, they are rude, quarrelsome, even openly hostile. Especially in the big cities, distrustfulness appears to be the only real constant.

This is an understandable attitude. The regular passenger on the Athens Metro knows that at peak times if one is too far from the doors of the carriage it'll be hard to get off in time at the required stop. The reasonable rule that ordinarily applies – those exiting have priority; those coming in wait their turn – ceases to operate. The force of those outside pushing to get on to the overcrowded train is so powerful that, even though you might be standing right by the door, it is sometimes hard to disembark. All the more so if you are standing five metres away and there are ten bodies between you and the exit. So then, if you want to spare yourself the distress and avoid all the elbowing with those just standing there rooted to the spot like statues or with those mounting an assault, best you stay as close to the doors as possible. Even if that means spending several minutes squashed like a sardine in a tin.

The situation in queues is not so different. The discipline of northern Europeans, which requires everyone to fall in line behind one another good naturedly and in a spirit of cooperation, seems to be completely absent here. The law of mistrustfulness holds sway. It is absolutely certain – as bitter experience has shown, sweeping away any inclination on your part to be courteous – it is absolutely certain that there will be no shortage of people who will try to circumvent the line of priority and steal your advantage.

For the more decent folks, or the more gallant, the choice here is a tough one. They will either have to be prepared to get into a personal quarrel with the cheaters every time – and such a quarrel is, alas, not painless, because these people are usually insolent and foul mouthed, all too ready to pick a fight – or they have to put up with them, tolerate them without protest, thus letting their inner voice chastise them for their cowardice and passivity. You will come across both in queues, yet the latter usually prevails. How much courage, how much stamina for the fight can one muster day in day out?

Only the sour faces attempting to appear impassive, or at best stoical, testify to the inner turmoil of those people. For some the day has already been laid to waste; they are aware that their retreat is not an act of superiority but a defeat, pure and simple, and one in which they did not stick up for themselves. And it's those same people that you will see unexpectedly explode on the next such occasion, with an intensity not warranted by the moment, although understandable in terms of accumulated irritation.

It is true that in recent years numbered priority slips have gone a long way to ameliorate the problem. In less formal situations, however, where it is not possible to take measures in advance, conditioned reflexes continue to rule the day. People in crowds almost automatically transform into a rabble. From easy-going neighbours to mutually antagonistic foes.

*

In 2011–15, at the height of the Greek crisis, passengers on public transport in Athens did not buy tickets. They had no need to. On getting off a bus or trolley bus there would always be someone disembarking who would give them theirs. Often you would spot the tickets right there, under your nose, unashamedly placed on top of the ticket machine. As they are good for ninety minutes after first use, if they change hands they can easily be used by more than one person. That sort of thing, naturally, goes against the rules, and if you get caught by a ticket inspector a hefty fine can ensue. But in those days nobody checked. The phenomenon became so widespread that to crack down on it the Metro management was forced to order ticket barriers for the entrances – and the number of illicit passengers declined sharply.

Such manifestations of 'solidarity' among strangers are not at all unusual. On the streets of Greece, for instance, a driver who has just spotted a police car stationed along the road will flash their lights as a warning to oncoming cars. The message is clear: careful, slow down, there's an ambush ahead! When a team from the tax office or health department or workplace inspectors are out doing their rounds, an alert goes out. Not only those who have

already undergone checks but all bystanders consider it their duty to notify others.

At first glance, these reactions must appear to run counter to those fuelled, as we saw, by the mutual mistrustfulness of Greeks and which foster a more combative behaviour. But things are not what they seem. Not only do they not belie that mistrustfulness but they are, in fact, its most resounding corroboration. Greeks trust state authorities even less than their fellow citizens. Hence, when they gang up with others against the state and its instruments, they are not prompted by a spirit of mutual help or support nor by a sense of justice or a desire to resist possible arbitrary abuses of power – not at all. Most often, with perfect awareness of what they are doing, they will rush to the aid of lawbreakers, whom they may well despise. Yet, their distrust of the state provides an even stronger impetus, and if they engage with others in small-scale conspiracies against authority they see it as a pre-emptive defence. Today or tomorrow, soon enough at any rate, they are bound to find themselves in the position of those they are now helping. Hence it is prudent to be able to count on their support, for them to know that they had their back so that they will do the same, in their turn, when the moment arrives.

*

Under these conditions, every form of collaboration with the authorities, every assistance offered them, is understandably considered reprehensible. Even those citizens who have a vested interest in reporting their neighbour – for encroaching on public space, perhaps, or making noise at an unacceptable hour – will do so rarely and unwillingly. All such reporting, even the most justifiable, is considered 'snitching', an immoral, traitorous act. The action of a Swiss citizen, who might call the municipal authorities to report a nearby neighbour for leaving his rubbish here, there and everywhere would be unthinkable for a Greek. In the face of a great common adversary, always the state, private differences pale into insignificance. In the face of the impersonal Leviathan that governs us, such is the general notion, we on this side need to be united. When the going gets tough, we need to stick together.

It goes without saying that there are historical precedents that explain this. For centuries Greeks lived under brutal regimes, under tyrannical authority. More than 120 armed revolts against Ottoman rule took place between 1453 and 1821 – that is, from the fall of Byzantium to the beginning of the war for national independence. There were dozens of bloody uprisings against the Franks, the western feudal nations who established themselves on Greek soil after 1204 and whose reign lasted for many centuries, especially in the islands. Under the conditions of foreign rule, insubordination against the state, revolt against it, deceiving it by any and every means, were not just practical necessities or morally laudable, they were a way of life; better still, a survival strategy.

Yet after independence, the recurring civil wars, political rifts and dictatorships perpetuated that sentiment. Irrespective of which party was in government, it faced the fanatical opposition of at least half the population and was chronically impeded by its unrelenting resistance. Historians refer to a *spirit*, a *culture of resistance*. And, as is well known, behaviours rooted in the culture of a place do not change easily. They survive atavistically even though the conditions that gave rise to them no longer obtain.

Let us think of the fetishistic relationship many Americans have with guns, their distrust of the state, the disdainful tone in which they utter the very word *government*. Certainly, all of that has history as its departure point, the risk-taking and anomie that accompanied frontier life in the Old West. Today, cut off from that point of origin, these traits fuel irrational violence, keeping alive a culture of private justice and bloodshed. Greeks – with the exception of the Cretans – do not share the American worship of the gun. Nevertheless they, too, feel continually threatened, the inhabitants of a savage and ongoing Wild West. And they have come up with their own means of defence, which can frequently also prove destructive.

*

A bank. The clerk is cantankerous, uncooperative, hard to please. In front of him a visibly intimidated customer with a folder on his knees crammed with papers, documents, certificates. Hurriedly, almost urgently, the customer obediently presents each one. None is sufficient. The clerk, cantankerous, uncooperative, hard to please, has dug his heels in. His entire body seems to emit a resounding 'Impossible!' The customer is sweating. Standing behind him, you can hear his breath is shallow. Laboured.

Suddenly, a voice. A colleague of the clerk passing through the big hall seems to recognise the customer. He pauses two paces behind him. Again he calls out his name. The two embrace, pleased and surprised in equal measure. The customer: 'I had no idea you worked here!' The colleague turns to the first clerk. 'Don't you know who this is?' The clerk evidently does not. But he finds out. The three are now chatting among themselves like friends from the old days, inseparable. As the customer takes his leave, the clerk, genial, affable, pleased, puts out his hand. There is no reason to come back, it goes without saying, he will handle the case himself. He can consider the matter taken care of.

*

Early hours of the morning. A large hospital in the capital. Intensive-care unit. Waiting room. At one end, weary and sleep deprived, the doctor in charge is explaining something to a patient's relatives. When he is done a young man (a son? a brother?) timidly hands him an envelope. The doctor at first pretends to refuse it. The young man insists. With a juggler's gesture that can be interpreted equally as a formal transaction and as sincere bashfulness, the doctor eventually gives in. Before leaving, he puts his hand on the young man's shoulder reassuringly. As if to say: I'm here.

Almost two hundred years after the declaration of political independence for modern Greece, the state built since then and, alongside it, every superior, abstract, 'impersonal' power, whether public or private, remains an adversary for its people. Nothing is more foreign to the Greeks than the notion that they may rely on or even look with confidence to the impartiality of the rule of law or the goodwill of an institution, a service, a company. On the contrary, the deeper they are immersed in daily survival (more the case for the weaker, more vulnerable social strata) the more the unshakeable awareness emerges: only the face-to-face relationship will guarantee you anything. Only a person you know or, at one remove, someone who knows someone you know, will be available on the phone tomorrow or the day after to provide an explanation for why you've not been treated right. Hence, that person is the only one you can go to from the start. The Greek is accountable only to his acquaintance; only an acquaintance can effectively appeal to his decency, can cause him to feel embarrassment and a sense of moral responsibility, and it is only to him he can look for support when the going gets tough.

A foreign observer might speak here of corruption. And, indeed, the European press spoke unanimously of our endemic corruption at the culmination of the crisis that brought the country to the verge of bankruptcy. This is how Greece was described even by the prime minister of the day: a corrupt country. But corruption is too shallow in meaning, too moralising, to describe this state of affairs. Money surreptitiously changing hands, bribery, paying a little something extra in exchange for 'inside help', 'greasing the wheel', expressions widely used both within and outside Greece, are not typical acts of corruption as a German or an American might understand them. They are symbolic acts of engagement which, as a gesture, far exceed the meaning of the specific act they regulate.

The patient, for instance, who willingly bribes his doctor, is not

simply buying the doctor off. The patient is doing something much deeper: founding a personal relationship based on complicity. The professional, impartial contact whom he does not trust, just as he does not trust in advance anyone's conscientiousness and competence, is here *personalised*. Through the envelope with bribe money, the doctor becomes his familiar, a real partner, providing the patient with some assurance that the doctor will do a good job – an assurance that no list of qualifications and no institutional controls can otherwise provide. The same with the bank clerk. Personal connection, the introduction, at the very least, by a common acquaintance, is additional insurance, an affirmation of closeness that can bend even the toughest bureaucracy. Even in a private credit institution, the standards are drastically lowered when the bond with the customer stops being formal and impersonal. With everything this implies ...

The parents paying a small fortune to their child's teacher for extracurricular tutoring, the shopkeeper pretending that he is saving his best stock for his customer ('Not from there! Let me get some for you!'), the publisher flattering his author, saying he will publish the book before even reading it, all of them personalise – that is, they imbue their professional relationship with the aspect, or merely the appearance, of a personal bond because they know, when everything's said and done, that is the only thing Greeks trust.

Indeed, in the absence of another mechanism for managing conflicts, with no confidence in the ability of laws and institutions to impart order, what assurance can one have apart from immediate personal contact? In an environment of constant mistrustfulness and unremitting quarrels, for trust to be born it needs to be immediate and experiential: personal. Only such bonds can soothe the tensions and bridge the gaps. Only they have the power to impart catharsis to the microdramas of haphazard life. 🐦

Paperchase

At the peak of the Greek crisis, a British woman decides to return to Greece to make her contribution to a country she loves and which has been her home for many years – but she hasn't reckoned with Greece's fearsome bureaucracy.

RACHEL HOWARD

Folders stacked high
in a public office in Athens.

In 2013 the first ever Greek cabinet minister to be jailed for corruption started a twenty-year sentence (of which he served five, being released in 2018 on health grounds). Akis Tsochatzopoulos received more than €50 million in kickbacks from the procurement of Russian missiles and German submarines during his tenure as defence minister. The Greek navy didn't get such a good deal: four of those submarines, purchased for €3 billion, were defective and have never been deployed.

Tsochatzopoulos's five-month trial in 2013 gripped the nation. It was Greece's version of the O.J. Simpson trial but with arms dealers and offshore dodges in place of celebrities and car chases. And Tsochatzopoulos – a heavyweight in the Panhellenic Socialist Movement (PASOK) – was convicted. He got twenty years in jail. His wife, daughter, ex-wife and over a dozen crooked cousins and cronies are also serving time.

As I watched the dramatic denouement of the trial on TV, I was flabbergasted. Not because justice had finally been served in a country where politicians and government officials seem to behave with impunity – but because Tsochatzopoulos's accountant, Euphrosyne Lambropoulou, was my accountant, too.

Hunched and handcuffed, the woman in court was hard to reconcile with the matronly, chain-smoking confidante I visited in a dingy basement office near the Athens law courts. Frosso, as everyone knew her, was usually found wedged behind her desk, spilling ash down her giant bosom as she flicked authoritatively through a jumble of ledgers and papers. Every two months I dutifully brought my own bulging file of receipts, along with my *blokaki* – my 'little book' of invoices – which had to be signed, stamped and submitted to the tax office along with VAT and income tax on whatever I had earned.

Often I would have to wait an hour, maybe two, passively smoking and eavesdropping on another client's tribulations with the taxman. Eventually my turn would come. After a lengthy preamble of grumble and gossip, Frosso would sift through my papers then tot up my dues. I would sigh theatrically and count out the cash, with a little extra for one of her long-suffering minions, who would traipse off to the tax office to collect more stamps and signatures on my behalf.

I never once received a receipt for Frosso's services – and I never dared ask for one – but I certainly didn't suspect this dowdy, Dickensian character of industrial-scale corruption. The truth is, I blindly followed

RACHEL HOWARD was born in London but moved to Greece at the age of five and has remained there ever since, at least in spirit. She regularly writes for *Condé Nast Traveler*, the *Guardian*, the *Telegraph* and *The Sunday Times*, mainly covering travel, food and design. She has written speeches for the former Greek minister for foreign affairs George Papandreou and is the author of two best-selling guides to London and a comic strip for children. Her latest publications include *Mykonos Muse*, published in 2018 by Assouline.

Frosso's financial advice without questioning it. If something seemed dubious, I preferred to turn a blind eye rather than grapple with the arcane Greek tax system. I like to think I followed the law to the letter. But, when I saw Frosso break down in court, I felt guilt by association – an accessory to a crime I had unwittingly condoned. I also felt sorry for Frosso's two young children, who occasionally did their homework in a corner of her office, drinking chocolate milk in a cloud of stale smoke.

Frosso had been recommended to me a decade earlier by one of my colleagues at the Greek Ministry of Foreign Affairs. At the time I was working as a speechwriter for the foreign minister (and later prime minister), George Papandreou. He was not one of Frosso's clients, but she claimed in court that she once had eleven PASOK ministers on her books as well as several TV pundits. They must have been quaking in their boots throughout her trial. When the prosecutor asked Frosso why she had covered up for Tsochatzopoulos, she said simply, 'I was in awe of him ... He was omnipotent.'

This is the crux of the problem with corruption in Greece: nobody expects to get caught. And if the fat cats are all fiddling the books, why shouldn't the rest of us? 'You know what they say about politics? The rotten fish stinks from the head,' an Athenian taxi driver will tell you, right before he tries to rip you off. On the islands, word that the tax inspector has arrived ripples through the bars before he or she has even stepped off the ferry. Doctors and dentists declare smaller incomes than bus drivers yet still expect a *fakelaki* – a 'little envelope' (stuffed with cash) – for their services.

There are signs that attitudes are changing from the grassroots up, as young, tech-savvy Greeks take matters into their own hands. Horrified that she had to bribe

'I PAID A BRIBE'

For her dissertation at Yale, Italian-Greek student Kristina Tremonti wanted to study the Greek system of *fakelaki*. The problem was that there were no data, although it was a widespread system, no one had ever studied it. She wrote her thesis on another subject, but a couple of years later, when the financial crisis broke out, she decided it was time to do something. She launched a project with the aim of helping her country fight one of the causes of the crisis, its rampant corruption. This was the origin of the website 'Edosa fakelaki' ('I paid a bribe'), edosafakelaki.org. The aim is not just to report those engaging in corruption but, above all, to convince the people of Greece that things can change: a section of the site is called 'I did not pay a bribe', and citizens are encouraged to be proud of the acts of resistance in which they suffered injustice for not playing the *fakelaki* game. The success of the project has led to the creation of similar sites in countries such as India, Pakistan, Kenya and Indonesia. Kristina Tremonti, who also worked as a consultant to the Greek government on the issue of corruption between 2015 and 2016, was included in the *Forbes* 2018 list of thirty Europeans under thirty who are fighting for better government. Her site has also finally supplied the data and statistics she was unable to source when she wanted to write her dissertation: how much do people ask for, in which regions of Greece is the phenomenon most prominent and in which sectors? At the top of the list are hospitals and the authorities that issue driving licences and construction permits.

a surgeon to perform emergency surgery on her ninety-year-old grandfather, Kristina Tremonti set up 'Edosa fakelaki' ('I paid a bribe'). It's a digital platform where people can anonymously name and shame the doctors, town planners, tax inspectors and driving instructors whose palms they have greased. Bringing these transactions into the open makes them both less taboo and, paradoxically, more shocking.

In theory, this body of evidence should also spur public prosecutors to take action; in practice, that hasn't happened. At the time of writing, more than 1,900 anonymous confessions of bribing officials had been made. Thirty-three whistle-blowers have posted complaints about specific individuals, which are passed directly to the authorities. Only one has been prosecuted. Perhaps that's why the recipients of bribes, who have their own online forum, generally appear unrepentant. 'Why did I take the money? Because I'm worth it,' they brag, with the irritating sense of entitlement of a L'Oréal model.

It's hard to change entrenched practices when everyone is complicit yet no one accepts responsibility. Ask Greeks why they collude with a culture of kickbacks, and they will usually shrug, 'It's just the way things are done here.' Or, more accurately, it's the only way to get things done.

God knows there have been enough articles riddled with stereotypes casting aspersions on the Greeks – especially in the British and German tabloids. And I realise I might sound like another sanctimonious foreigner, wagging my finger and telling Greece to pull its socks up. In fact, I've carved out a career as a professional cheerleader for Greece, the beloved country where I've lived on and off since I was five. But brushes with officialdom can drive even the most diehard philhellene to despair.

Just to illustrate my point, a few years ago I paid off the mortgage on my little flat in Athens. Before I could celebrate I had to jump through several hoops to remove the bank from the title deeds. For days I scuttled between the bank, the tax office and the land registry. Finally, I reached the last hurdle: a lawyer appointed by the bank would meet me at the central Athens law courts, where we would both solemnly swear before a member of the judiciary that my flat was indeed mine.

At the appointed time a glamorous blonde in shiny heels met me in a shabby corridor with peeling paint. I signed some documents, and then we waited. And waited. There was no queue or ticketing system; just a crush of people aimlessly wondering when they might get out of there and on with their lives. Eventually we were summoned before an imperious official who stamped my papers with a flurry of thumps, under the mournful gaze of a nicotine-stained saint. I thanked the lawyer and asked her how much I owed.

'Three hundred euros. Two hundred if you don't want a receipt,' she replied without batting a heavily made-up eyelid.

Reluctantly, and foolishly, I paid the lower fee. The irony of a lawyer breaking the law, right there in the courthouse, was not lost on me. For weeks I fumed and cursed myself for playing the game. That's when I knew it was time for me to leave Greece – at least for a while.

I moved to London, had a baby, found freelance work. But Greece never really left me. I returned as often as I could. I wrote good-news stories about Greek hotels, startups and solidarity movements. I watched the country's sovereign debt crisis snowball from a safe distance, but I couldn't detach myself from it. Friends and family in Greece struggled to make sense of the hysterical politics and struggled to

'The irony of a lawyer breaking the law, right there in the courthouse, was not lost on me.'

make ends meet as salaries and pensions were slashed, taxes spiked and businesses went bust. Public services broke down, tensions flared up. The crisis – the term that's still used to describe Greece's predicament, although it has dragged on for a decade – was brutal, chaotic, divisive. The old order was unravelling, but the establishment refused to let go.

At first I optimistically assumed there would be a silver lining to the brutal conditions attached to the bailout: corruption would be flushed out into the open. Since 2008 eight governments across the political spectrum have come and gone in quick succession. None has had the nerve to take on those with vested interests, the oligarchs and union leaders who elected them in exchange for lucrative government contracts or jobs for life.

Greece's creditors have made matters worse. You can't starve an economy back into recovery – especially when most of the bailout money goes to pay off existing loans. The heavy-handed austerity imposed by the troika (the IMF, the European Commission and the European Central Bank) has pushed the middle class into poverty and stoked the shadow economy. Repeatedly raising taxes on pensioners, low-income workers and the self-employed hasn't increased revenues because people simply can't afford to pay.

Figures from 2018 show that Greek taxpayers owed €182.5 billion to the Greek state, not including the many tens of billions due in penalties. More than 3.7 million taxpayers – around 60 per cent of Greeks with taxable income – were in arrears. The government started seizing assets without warning and freezing the pensions and benefits of those in debt to the tax authorities.

The Greek tax system doesn't exactly encourage compliance. In recent years somewhere between forty-eight and well in excess of two thousand new tax laws have been passed – depending on which newspaper you read. It's hard to know whether you're breaking the rules when the rules change almost weekly. Those who scrupulously pay their taxes end up feeling like schmucks. As one law-abiding friend who runs a construction business ruefully told me, 'The only way to survive now is to be illegal.'

In an effort to clamp down on tax evasion, in 2013 the Ministry of Finance decreed that all tax returns must be filed online – a radical move for which both state and citizens were completely unprepared. Internet penetration in Greece is around 72 per cent, among the lowest in Europe. Many tax inspectors don't even have access to a computer, never mind the shepherds and fishermen in Greece's remote highlands and islands. Under this new-fangled system you have to apply for a unique tax reference number online – and then wait in line at the tax office to collect it in person. Once you've submitted your digital tax return you have to go back to the tax office to hand over all the supporting paperwork.

There are other hurdles to overcome. If you're self-employed (like 33.5 per cent of Greeks), your social security contributions would go up every year, regardless of your

Citizens queuing at the Athens offices of DEI, the national power company.

THE MINISTRY OF CORRUPTION
AND MONEY LAUNDERING

Akis Tsochatzopoulos, a founding member of the Greek socialist party PASOK, was elected to parliament for the first time in 1981 and notched up ministerial posts in every government until 2004, including a spell as minister of defence between 1996 and 2001. In 2010, a few days before parliament approved a series of austerity measures, the Greek newspapers accused Tsochatzopoulos's wife of having bought a lemon-yellow neoclassical-style house on one of the most expensive streets in Athens for a million euros from an offshore company. Over the next few months new accusations piled up: irregularities in his declarations of income and assets, corruption and money laundering. Tsochatzopoulos was expelled from the party,

and a year later, at the age of seventy-two, he was arrested. He was accused of receiving bribes worth tens of millions of euros relating to the purchase of Russian missile systems and German submarines, as well as having set up a series of offshore companies and Swiss bank accounts to launder his money. In 2013 he was sentenced to the maximum term of twenty years in prison, which was then reduced by a year. Sixteen other defendants were also found guilty, including his wife and daughter. He was released in 2018 after just five years because of severe health problems. As a slim consolation, his successor at the Ministry of Defence, Yiannos Papantoniou, who was in office from 2001 to 2004, was arrested a few months later on very similar charges relating to a contract for the modernisation of naval frigates.

CORRUPTION

Despite having risen by nine points since 2012, Greece remains in penultimate place in the EU in the Corruption Perception Index and sixty-seventh in the world.

Global position and score

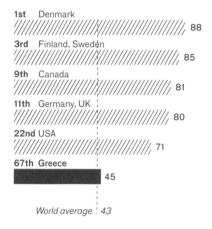

1st Denmark
////////////////////////////////////// 88

3rd Finland, Sweden
////////////////////////////////////// 85

9th Canada
////////////////////////////////////// 81

11th Germany, UK
////////////////////////////////////// 80

22nd USA
////////////////////////////////// 71

67th Greece
███████████ 45

World average 43

SOURCE: TRANSPARENCY INTERNATIONAL (2018)

PUBLIC ADMINISTRATION

The European Quality of Government Index, developed by the Quality of Government Institute at the University of Gothenburg and funded by the European Commission, evaluates the standards of institutions in EU countries. Greece comes in third from bottom; the UK is seventh from top.

Position in the EU and average score

1st Finland
////////////////////////////////////// 1.93

2nd Sweden, Denmark
////////////////////////////////////// 1.92

6th Germany
////////////////////////////////// 1.69

7th UK
//////////////////////////////// 1.67

11th France
////////////////////////// 1.33

23rd Italy
/////////// 0.42

26th Greece
███ 0.24

28th Bulgaria
/ 0.04

SOURCE: QUALITY OF GOVERNMENT INSTITUTE (2017)

actual income – until this law was finally replaced with an income-based national insurance system in 2018. In Greece, where the minimum wage is €684 a month, I was paying around €400 a month in national insurance. You also have to pay VAT up front, regardless of whether your clients have, in fact, paid you. When the system is irrational and unfair, people inevitably work around it.

Undeterred, at the height of the financial crisis a few years ago I embarked on my own personal mission to boost the Greek economy. A friend convinced me to apply for a job with a government agency promoting tourism and investment in Greece. First, I had to complete a complicated tender to make sure I was qualified for the job – a good sign that public money was being spent, perhaps not wisely, but well. My application was successful. A one-year contract landed in my inbox. In all the years I've worked in Greece, I'd never had an official contract before. Wow, I thought, things really have changed since I've been gone.

Of course, nothing is ever that simple – at least not when it comes to Greek bureaucracy. Before the board of directors could approve my contract I would have to submit over a dozen documents from the Greek authorities. I scanned the list. I didn't owe any taxes or national insurance. I didn't need a licence to practise my profession. I'd never owned a company or employed any staff, never been bankrupt,

'I deployed the tried-and-tested tactic of grilling a weary functionary about her family; by the time I'd heard all about her precocious granddaughter and mother with Alzheimer's, my forms had been fast-tracked.'

gone into liquidation or been suspended for professional misconduct. I didn't need a residence permit. I didn't have a criminal record. I had never been part of a criminal organisation, accepted a bribe or been convicted of fraud or money laundering.

I called the HR department of my prospective employer.

'None of these provisos apply to me,' I said.

'Sorry, we still need the evidence to prove it.'

So I hired a lawyer and gritted my teeth. I waited with nervous immigrants at the Ministry of Justice, where a browbeaten apparatchik was single-handedly fielding all requests. I rode wheezing elevators up and down the tax office, trying to figure out which department was where and who needed to stamp what. I was bullied by a tax inspector while he baldly negotiated a job for his son-in-law with a stooge. I was consoled by a Romanian accountant whose experience of communism had taught her to handle beadledom with cheerful stoicism. I deployed the tried-and-tested tactic of grilling a weary functionary about her family; by the time I'd heard all about her precocious granddaughter and mother with Alzheimer's, my forms had been fast-tracked.

Scuffles broke out between shiny-suited plaintiffs at the law courts, a compound of cryptically numbered buildings where giant bundles of tattered files teetered on every available surface. There was no sign

of the government's digitisation drive here. Even with precise instructions from my lawyer the procedure for legalising documents was completely (perhaps deliberately) impenetrable.

This is roughly how it works:

1) locate the right building;

2) find the right office – none is signposted;

3) track down the relevant form amid countless stacks of paper;

4) fill out the barely legible, wonkily printed form;

5) run downstairs to buy official stamps from one of the shifty hawkers loitering outside;

6) run back upstairs;

7) return the form to the correct dog-eared cardboard box lined up on the counter;

8) take a scrap of paper with the collection date;

9) repeat, *ad infinitum*; and, finally, return on the appointed day to pick up your rubber-stamped forms, praying that none has gone astray. (Wishful thinking.)

I queued for what felt like days at the national insurance office. Like all government buildings in Greece it had a particular smell of neglect and nostalgia – a physical manifestation of an anachronistic administration desperately in need of modernisation. The walls were scuffed, the leatherette chairs ripped. Apart from overflowing ashtrays (smoking is, theoretically, forbidden in all public buildings in Greece) the

'Apart from overflowing ashtrays (smoking is, theoretically, forbidden in all public buildings in Greece) the only interior decoration was a laminated icon pinned to a notice board explaining how to claim unemployment benefits.'

only interior decoration was a laminated icon pinned to a notice board explaining how to claim unemployment benefits. And, of course, the usual crude graffiti, expressing something between ennui and anguish: 'UFO, Wake Up!'; 'VASANIZOMAI' (I am tortured) – a feeling I recognised when the clerk broke the news that my national insurance file had randomly been transferred to another office.

So I raced across town and queued again, only to be told by a poker-faced official that the file had been 'mislaid'. Although my digital file on her computer screen showed that my accounts were up to date, she couldn't issue me with a statement to that effect until I could produce the documentation to prove it.

'But I don't have the file. You do.'

'Well, it's not here.'

'Then can you help me find it?'

'How am I supposed to do that?'

'I have no idea.'

'Neither do I.'

'How about calling the other office to see whether they still have it?'

'That's not my responsibility.'

'So what do you want me to do? I can't get paid unless you give me that piece of paper.'

'I can't help you unless you can find your file.'

I wheedled, cajoled, demanded to see the manager, flew into a rage and finally burst into tears. Nobody seemed the least bit ruffled by my histrionics. Eventually I got the statement I needed. Afterwards I noticed it was only valid for a week.

In the end it took three weeks and several hundred euros to get all my papers in order. My triumph was short lived. The agency's lawyer called to inform me that, as I was not a Greek citizen, I would have to repeat the whole procedure in the United Kingdom.

'But most of these documents don't even exist in England,' I protested.

'In that case,' she replied, 'you must go to a notary and sign a solemn declaration. Then all your documents must be legalised with The Hague Apostille and officially translated into Greek. If you have any further questions, call the British Embassy in Athens. Goodbye.'

These Kafkaesque scenes are part of everyday life for Greeks, whether they're trying to pay their taxes, claim benefits, apply for permits and licences or register properties, births or deaths. Red tape, recession and (until they were lifted in September 2019) capital controls, are slowly suffocating entrepreneurialism. Caught between sclerotic politics and economic paralysis, hundreds of thousands of bright and brilliant Greeks are either unemployed or working abroad. Meanwhile, the deep state has dug in its heels, stubbornly resisting reforms.

The faceless British bureaucracy wasn't much of an improvement. At least in Greece you can argue with a real person. In England I could only yell obscenities at automated messages on extortionate 'helplines' until the hold music drove me so crazy I hung up.

Five weeks (thanks due to Her Majesty's Revenue and Customs) and several hundred pounds later, I finally handed over all the British paperwork to my new employer. By this time I'd already been working for two months without being paid because my contract hadn't been signed. A month later, after much pestering and pleading, I received one month's salary 'as a gesture of goodwill'. I'd have to wait for the rest, as EU funds were not forthcoming. Eventually I told the HR department that I would have to put the job on hold until the money came through. A few weeks later, instead of a pay cheque, I received a termination agreement.

After eight months of begging and bullying my former employer I finally got the money I was owed. Four years later I'm still trying to track down my missing file at the national insurance agency. Without it I can't officially close my books in Greece. And I need closure, you see. Just like everyone else in Greece for whom crisis has become a way of life. ✒

The Island
of Long Life

On the island of Ikaria, life
is sweet ... and very, very long.
So what is the islanders' secret?

ANDREW ANTHONY

G regoris Tsahas has smoked a packet of cigarettes every day for seventy years. High up in the hills of Ikaria, in his favourite café, he draws on what must be around his half-millionth cigarette. I tell him smoking is bad for the health, and he gives me an indulgent smile, which suggests he's heard the line before. He's a hundred years old and, aside from appendicitis, has never known a day of illness in his life.

Tsahas has short-cropped white hair, a robustly handsome face and a bone-crushing handshake. He says he drinks two glasses of red wine a day, but, on closer interrogation, he concedes that, like many other drinkers, he has underestimated his consumption by a couple of glasses.

The secret of a good marriage, he tells me, is never to return drunk to your wife. He's been married for sixty years. 'I'd like another wife,' he says. 'Ideally one about fifty-five.'

Tsahas is known at the café as a bit of a gossip and a joker. He goes there twice a day. It's a kilometre's walk from his house over uneven, sloping terrain. That's four hilly kilometres a day. Not many people half his age manage that far in Britain.

In Ikaria, a Greek island in the far east of the Mediterranean, about fifty kilometres from the Turkish coast, characters such as Gregoris Tsahas are not exceptional. With its beautiful coves, rocky cliffs, steep valleys and broken canopy of scrub and olive groves, Ikaria looks similar to any number of other Greek islands. But there is one vital difference: people here live much longer than the population on other islands and on the mainland. In fact, people here live on average ten years longer than those in the rest of Europe and America – around one in three Ikarians lives into their nineties. Not only that, they also have much lower rates of cancer and heart disease, suffer significantly less depression and dementia, maintain a sex life into old age and remain physically active deep into their nineties. What is the secret of Ikaria? What do its inhabitants know that the rest of us don't?

*

The island is named after Icarus, the young man in Greek mythology who flew too close to the sun and plunged into the sea, according to legend, close to Ikaria. Thoughts of plunging into the sea are very much in my mind as the propeller plane from Athens comes in to land. There is a fierce wind blowing – the island is renowned for its wind – and the aircraft appears to stall as it turns to make its final descent, tipping this way and that until, at the last moment, the

ANDREW ANTHONY is an investigative reporter and journalist who has written for the *Observer* since 1993 as well as contributing to the *Guardian*, *Vogue* and the *Telegraph*. His articles cover an extremely diverse range of subjects: politics, crime, sport, literature, television and pop culture. In 2001 Yellow Jersey Press published his essay *On Penalties*.

"'Ikaria is still an isolated island, with few tourists, which means that, especially in the villages in the north where the highest longevity rates have been recorded, life is largely unaffected by the Westernised way of living.'"

pilot pulls upwards and returns to Athens. There aren't any ferries, owing to a strike. 'They're always on strike,' an Athenian back at the airport tells me.

Stranded in Athens for the night, I discover that a fellow thwarted passenger is Dan Buettner, author of a book called *The Blue Zones* (National Geographic, 2012), which details the five small areas in the world where the population outlive the American and western European average by around a decade: Okinawa in Japan, Sardinia, the Nicoya Peninsula in Costa Rica, Loma Linda in California and Ikaria.

Tall and athletic, 52-year-old Buettner, who used to be a long-distance cyclist, looks a picture of well-preserved youth. He is a fellow with *National Geographic* magazine and became interested in longevity while researching Okinawa's aged population. He tells me there are several other passengers on the plane who are interested in Ikaria's exceptional demographics. 'It would have been ironic, don't you think,' he notes drily, 'if a group of people looking for the secret of longevity crashed into the sea and died.'

Chatting to locals on the plane the following day, I learn that several have relations who are centenarians. One woman says her aunt is 111. The problem for demographers with such claims is that they are often very difficult to prove one way or the other. Going back to Methuselah, history is studded with exaggerations of age. In the last century longevity became yet another battleground in the cold war: the Soviet authorities let it be known that

people in the Caucasus were living deep into their hundreds, but subsequent studies have shown these claims lacked evidential foundation.

Since then various societies and populations have reported advanced ageing, but few are able to supply convincing proof. 'I don't believe Korea or China,' Buettner says. 'I don't believe the Hunza Valley in Pakistan. None of those places has good birth certificates.'

However, Ikaria does. It has also been the subject of a number of scientific studies. Aside from the demographic surveys that Buettner helped organise, there was also the University of Athens's Ikaria Study. One of its members, Dr Christina Chrysohoou, a cardiologist at the university's medical school, found that the Ikarian diet featured a lot of beans and not much meat or refined sugar. The locals also feast on locally grown and wild greens, some of which contain ten times more antioxidants than are found in red wine, as well as potatoes and goat's milk.

Chrysohoou thinks the food is distinct from that eaten on other Greek islands with lower life expectancy. 'Ikarians' diet may have some differences from other islands' diets,' she says. 'The Ikarians drink a lot of herb tea and small quantities of coffee; daily calorie consumption is not high. Ikaria is still an isolated island, with few tourists, which means that, especially in the villages in the north where the highest longevity rates have been recorded, life is largely unaffected by the Westernised way of living.'

THE PASSENGER   Andrew Anthony

A bar in Mytilene, Lesbos.

The Island of Long Life

But she also refers to research that suggests the Ikarian habit of taking afternoon naps may help extend life. One extensive study of Greek adults showed that regular napping reduced the risk of heart disease by almost 40 per cent. What's more, Chrysohoou's preliminary studies revealed that 80 per cent of Ikarian males between the ages of sixty-five and a hundred were still having sex, and, of those, a quarter did so with 'good duration' and 'achievement'. 'We found that most males between sixty-five and eighty-eight reported sexual activity, but after the age of ninety very few continued to have sex.'

*

In a small village called Nas at the western end of Ikaria's north shore is Thea's Inn, a bustling guesthouse run by Thea Parikos, an American-Ikarian who returned to her roots and married a local. Ever since Buettner arrived with his research team here a few years back Thea's Inn has been a sort of base camp for anyone looking to study the island's older population.

It's a good introduction to Ikarian life, if only because the dining table always seems to bear a jug of homemade red wine and dishes made from garden-grown vegetables. Every household we enter over the next four days, even at the shortest notice, invariably produces the same appetising hospitality. Yet Ikarians are far from wealthy. The island has not escaped the Greek economic crisis, and around 40 per cent of its inhabitants are unemployed. Nearly everyone grows their own food and many produce their own wine.

There is also a strong tradition of solidarity among Ikarians. During the Second World War, when the island was occupied by the Italians and the Germans, there was substantial loss of life through starvation – some estimates put the death toll at 20 per cent of the population. It's been speculated that one of the reasons for Ikarians' longevity is a Darwinian effect of survival of the fittest.

After the war thousands of communists and leftists were exiled to the island, bringing an ideological underpinning to the Ikarians' instinct to share. As one of the island's few doctors told Buettner, 'It's not a "me" place, it's an "us" place.'

Nearly all elderly Ikarians have a story of suffering, although few are keen to tell it. Kostas Sponsas lost a leg in Albania, when he was blown up by a German shell. He was saved by fellow Ikarians, without whose help he would have died from loss of blood. '"Be strong," they told me,' he says. '"Have courage!"' He turns one hundred this month and is more mobile than many younger men with two legs. Each day he pays a visit to the office of the shop he set up decades ago. 'If I feel tired, I read. It rests my mind.' He was determined not to get depressed after losing his leg as a young man, instead remembering his grandfather's advice. 'He used to say to me, "Be grateful that nothing worse has happened."'

In terms of longevity it was wise counsel. Depression, sadness, loneliness, stress – they can and do take a decade off our lives. Sponsas's own tips for a long life are that he never eats food fried with butter, always sleeps well and with the window open, avoids eating too much meat, drinks herb tea – mint or sage – and makes sure to have a couple of glasses of red wine with his food.

Sponsas's son, a large middle-aged man with a broad smile, is with him when I visit, fixing a broken door. Family is a vital part of Ikarian culture, and every old person I visit has children and grandchildren actively involved in their lives. Eleni Mazari, an estate agent on the island and a repository of local knowledge, says, 'We

Maria, eighty-five, still runs her grocery store.

keep the old people with us. There is an old people's home, but the only people there are those who have lost all their family. It would shame us to put an old person in a home. That's the reason for longevity.'

Sponsas agrees. 'To have your family around you makes you feel stronger and more secure.'

Just a minute's walk from his house in the picturesque port of Evdilos is the spotless home of Evangelia Karnava. In Ikaria, if you ask people their age, the answer they give is the year they were born. Karnava, a tiny but formidable woman, was born in 1916. She radiates a fierce energy, gesticulating like a politician on the stump. She lost two baby girls to starvation during the war, but she's not someone haunted by tragedy. Instead she speaks of her three children, seven grandchildren, four great-grandchildren and her great-great-grandchild. 'I'm going to live to be 115,' she tells me. 'My grandmother was 107.'

She certainly looks as if she's fit for a good few years yet. She cleans her own flat and goes shopping every day. What's her secret? She pours out glasses of Coca-Cola for her guests. 'I can't live without it!' she says.

Buettner appreciates the irony. He has been studying the diets of the various blue zones he's visited for clues to a healthier lifestyle that can be transported to post-industrial Western societies. Cigarettes and Coca-Cola were not meant to be part of the programme.

*

The term blue zone was first coined by Buettner's colleague, the Belgian demographer Michel Poulain. 'He was drawing blue circles on a map in Sardinia and then referring to the area inside the circle as the blue zone,' Buettner says. 'When we started working together I extended it

THE GOOD LORD HELPS THOSE WHO HELP THEMSELVES

In a sunny corner of California, a hundred kilometres east of Los Angeles, is the community of Loma Linda, where life revolves around the Seventh-Day Adventist Church, which was founded in 1840 and accounts for around ten thousand of the world's longest-living people. As in other blue zones, areas of the world where people live longer than average, the longevity of the Californian Adventists is down to many factors, which, in this case, are linked to their faith. Their doctrine emphasises health: most Adventists follow a vegetarian diet, do regular physical exercise and avoid smoking, alcohol and fast food. The body is a temple, the instrument through which they honour God, in an intersection of religion, science and physical well-being. (Seventh-Day Adventists were pioneers in the creation of meat alternatives, such as veggie burgers and hotdogs.) And then if you consider that most Adventists have friends in their own community, you can understand how they find it so easy to follow a lifestyle that might seem excessively restrictive. Life in Loma Linda is relatively stress free because it involves so much communal activity: people do not work on the Sabbath, and for many of them charity work is a priority; family ties are strong, and the elderly are rarely sent to nursing homes.

Stratis, eighty-five, in his carpentry workshop.

During the Civil War of 1946–9 tens of thousands of political opponents, most of them communists, were deported to islands in the Aegean. Some were imprisoned in concentration camps built on uninhabited islands, such as the Makronissos camp (known as Purgatory) or the women-only Trikeri camp, where they were forced to live in inhuman conditions and suffer torture at the hands of their armed guards. Others were sent to inhabited but poor islands without the necessary means for survival: the exiles' living conditions depended to a large extent on an island's resources, their ability to organise themselves and their relationship with the locals. The unusual thing about Ikaria, to which around thirteen thousand deportees were sent, as against an original population of fewer than ten thousand, was the hospitality extended by the locals to the exiles, which was, in part, a consequence of a tradition of resistance that over time has earned the island the nickname of *Kokkinos Vrachos*, or Red Rock: in 1912 it freed itself from Ottoman occupation and proclaimed itself the Free State of Ikaria, which lasted for five months before it was annexed by the Kingdom of Greece. During the Italian and German occupation the population hid British soldiers who had been trapped on the island, and after 8 September 1943 did the same for Italian soldiers. When the exiles arrived, the islanders welcomed them into their homes, developing a way of life based on solidarity and cooperation. The island still retains its political leanings: the Communist Party, which has around a 5 per cent vote share nationally, has over 30 per cent support on Ikaria, the highest anywhere in Greece.

to Okinawa, Costa Rica and Ikaria. If you google it now, it's entered the lexicon as a demographically confirmed geographical area where people live measurably longer.' So what does it take to qualify? 'It's a variation,' Buettner says. 'It's either the highest centenarian rate, so the most centenarians per thousand, or it has the highest life expectancy at middle age.'

All the blue zones are slightly austere environments where life has traditionally required hard work. But they also tend to be very social, and none more so than Ikaria. At the heart of the island's social scene is a series of 24-hour festivals, known as *panigiri*, which all age groups attend. They last right through the night, and the centre-pieces are mass dances in which everyone – teenagers, parents, the elderly, young children – takes part. Kostas Sponsas tells me he no longer has the energy to go on until dawn; he will now usually take his leave by 2 a.m.

One evening the island's star violin player, whom we met at Gregoris Tsahas's favourite café, invites Buettner, me and several others back to his house to hear him play. He says he often grows exhausted while performing at festivals, but the energy and enthusiasm of the people keep him going. He plays some traditional folk tunes, full of passion and yearning and heart-rending beauty, and mentions with pride that Mikis Theodorakis, best known internationally for composing the music for the 1964 film *Zorba the Greek*, was among the leftists exiled on the island in the late 1940s. Theodorakis later recalled the experience with pleasure. How could it be? he asked. The answer was simple: the beauty of the island combined with the warmth of the locals. 'They risked their lives to be generous to us, something that helped us more than anything bear the burden of this hardship.'

'I ask a number of men in their nineties and hundreds if they do any keep-fit exercises. The answer is always the same: "Yes, digging the earth."'

One of the things Buettner has found that unites the elderly inhabitants of all the blue zones is that they are unintentionally old: they didn't set out to extend their lives. 'Longevity happened to these people,' he says. 'The centenarians didn't all of a sudden at forty say, "I'm going to live to be a hundred; I'm going to start getting exercise and eating these ingredients." It ensues from their surroundings. So my argument is that the environmental components of places such as Ikaria are portable if you pay attention. And the value proposition in the real world is maybe a decade more life expectancy. It's not living to one hundred. But I think the real benefit is that the same things that yield this healthy longevity also yield happiness.'

I ask a number of men in their nineties and hundreds if they do any keep-fit exercises. The answer is always the same: 'Yes, digging the earth.' Nikos Fountoulis, for example, is a 93-year-old who looks twenty years younger. He still has a small-holding in the hills of the island's interior. Each morning he goes out at 8 a.m. to feed his animals and tend his garden. He used to dig charcoal as a younger man. 'I never thought about getting old,' he says. 'I feel good. I feel ninety-three, but on Ikaria that's OK.'

*

The island's greatest charm is that it is an unselfconscious sort of place. That could soon change: the spread of tourism is bound to have an effect. The island is protected by its remoteness and limited access but is now at the mercy of blue-zone tourists, those relentless hordes of blue-rinsed travellers looking for the secret elixir of eternal life. Buettner is doubtful that his book will lead to planeloads of Floridian retirees crowding the island. 'What are they going to do?' he asks. 'They're not going to be able to descend upon the woman milking a goat.'

On the day I leave Ikaria I come across a man in a baseball cap sitting in a chair outside his house in Evdilos. He is called Vangelis Koutis, and he's ninety-seven. He had left the island when he was fourteen to join the merchant navy. He travelled all over the world, including to Middlesbrough in the UK, and finally settled in Canada. But, like many Ikarians, he decided to return home in later life, in his case when he was seventy. I ask what brought him back.

'Fresh air,' he says, 'the best climate in the world and the friendliest people I've ever met.'

With that he returns to enjoying the sunshine on a beautiful spring afternoon. It's hard to imagine Middlesbrough or many other places offering quite so pleasant a time for a man in his nineties. Life in the blue zone is good. And that may be the real secret of why it's also so long. ✒

Greeks Bearing Gifts

ALEXANDER CLAPP

During the crisis Greece fell into the hands of a new generation of oligarchs who amassed fortunes and took advantage of the emergency to snap up strategic parts of the country; a story of savage privatisations, shady dealings and the shadow of the Kremlin.

It is hard to understand how the Greek state works without understanding the power held by a small circle of industrialists and financiers concentrated mostly in Athens. They are the oligarchs. Many inherited their fortunes or first accumulated them at sea, where their fleets collectively comprise the largest merchant marine on earth. Then they pivoted into other spheres. Some moved into construction. Others set up banks. Most own a chain of hotels or collect property. Those with ships already pay the minimal tax rate in Greece owing to legislation passed by the 1967–74 military junta that allows their capital to be assessed in shipping tonnage rather than profits. Sometimes looping their industries through Cypriot or Liberian shell companies, oligarchs nevertheless remain based in Greece, where they extract additional advantages – bailouts courtesy of the Greek taxpayer, lucrative state contracts – through political blackmail.

With every new government that takes power in Athens, the oligarchs threaten to take away the jobs they provide and the cash they push into the political system should any attempt be made to audit their assets or tax them effectively. In the last three decades not a single major party has run for election in Greece that did not vow to break the collective power of this group of men; no single one has attempted to do so once elected. What is more, oligarchs in Greece are able to control the narrative that's told about them because there is hardly a newspaper, television channel or magazine in the country that is not owned by one of them. The power of the oligarchs is such that press outfits within – and outside – the country have many legal and financial incentives not to call them out by name.

One might think that a decade of economic turmoil would cripple the power of Greece's 'great men', but instead the crisis has only flushed the country with greater flows of foreign capital and more opportunities for asset seizure. Retrospectively, much of what once seemed innocuous investment in Greece has since proved suspect. In 2016 the China Ocean Shipping Company acquired the port of Piraeus, the largest cargo container terminal in the eastern Mediterranean, for the equivalent of two-weeks'-worth of debt relief; since then, one instance of purported smuggling and customs evasion by the nascent Chinese mafia in Greece has followed another. Four years earlier half of Flisvos Marina near Athens, Greece's largest marina, was sold off to Ferit Şahenk, at the time Turkey's richest man, who, in 2016, picked up the Athens Hilton – his fortune aggrandised in the interim by the tightening of his allegiance to President Erdoğan following the failed 2016 coup in Turkey.

The crisis has also ushered in a different species of plutocrat, a new crop of moneyed elites. Call them vulture oligarchs. Many were not even born in Greece but have swooped down on the country in the last decade to pick off swathes of property and industrial businesses for pittances. The provenance of most of their capital is at best suspect, at worst blatantly illegal. The family of Dimitris Melissanidis, an oil tycoon with roots in North Ossetia who has been caught up in allegations of smuggling fuel and has provided the US Sixth Fleet in

ALEXANDER CLAPP is an Athens-based journalist whose articles on Greece, the Balkans and eastern Europe have appeared in the *London Review of Books*, the *New Left Review* and *The Times Literary Supplement*.

the Mediterranean with its oil since 2003, now lords over OPAP, the former Greek-state-owned gambling conglomerate. A handful of other barons – Dimitrios Copelouzos, Spiros Latsis – have taken over airports and huge chunks of coastline. Each of these figures presents exaggerated versions of what Greeks call *diaploki*, the nefarious intertwining of government and private interests that austerity has deepened, not dismantled.

Ivan Ignatyevich Savvidis is the parvenu of this group. He has played many unusual roles in his life – one of the great tobacco tycoons of Eurasia, a member of Russia's Duma, a confidant of Vladimir Putin – but it is his latest that is now setting off alarm bells throughout Europe. Since the onset of the economic crisis he has effectively seized personal ownership of significant sections of Thessaloniki, Greece's second city and the country's maritime gateway to the Balkans. The fire sale of old state assets – an auctioning process ordained by the European Union as part of its enforcement of economic austerity but which has become overwhelmingly rigged by vested political interests within Greece – has given Savvidis a rare opportunity to invest hundreds of millions of euros into his ancestral homeland. A football team, a grand luxury hotel, a tobacco conglomerate, a water-bottling company, a string of beach resorts, a television station, a trio of newspapers, great stretches of coastline and blocks of Thessaloniki property, the port of Thessaloniki and its industrial warehouses – these are just a few of the holdings that Savvidis has quietly acquired in the last decade. The buying spree has even given rise to a strange new coinage

splashing across the newspaper headlines and streets of his adopted city: *Ivanaptiksi*, 'prosperity emanating from Ivan'.

This slow-motion conquest, taking place hundreds of kilometres from Athens in a city that makes few international headlines, has now begun to raise serious questions. How has a man worth US$1.9 billion on paper invested close to half of that amount in Greece in less than a decade? In late 2017 allegations were openly raised by the European press, along with concerns publicly voiced by the US ambassador in Athens, to suggest that Ivan Savvidis was not what he appeared to be: masquerading as the financial saviour of Thessaloniki, the theory runs, he is, in fact, a conduit of Putinist interests in the Aegean.

Seen in this light, virtually all of Savvidis's business deals and public undertakings in Greece seem to serve Moscow's agenda. His dealings with the centre-right New Democracy Party – marrying off his niece to its general secretary, pitting its various clans against one another, peeling off the loyalties of its elected constituents through purported bribery all across northern Greece – appear to be an effort to sow division within the party most keen on Greece's continued membership of the European Union. His purchase of Thessaloniki's port seems like a move to stymie NATO's naval access to the Balkans, a region at the convergence of Russian and American spheres of influence. The millions of euros Savvidis has donated to the monasteries of Mount Athos for the construction of new churches act simultaneously as a Russian investment of soft power in a no-man's land of international authority and financial transparency.

These allegations may just as easily be false, the by-product of geopolitical conspiracy mongering and Russia-paranoia gone rogue. It would hardly be the first

'The typical Greek oligarch is not a self-made man. His family has been wealthy or siphoning money out of the public coffers or both for generations. He inherits a fleet of ships, invests minimally within Greece then blackmails whichever government happens to be in power.'

time the West's cottage industry of anti-Putinism has the paradoxical effect of making Russia's reach seem far greater than it actually is. But, in any case, the remarkable rise of Ivan Savvidis to a place of political prominence exposes an uncomfortable truth about the present course of the Greek state. Born in Georgia, enriched in Russia, Savvidis is an uncanny personification of Greece's regression from a western-European-style state – the type of country austerity was supposed to finally hammer into existence – into something much more familiar to observers of the post-Soviet terrain.

The most important thing to understand about Savvidis is that he is nothing like the oligarchs Greece has seen before. The typical Greek oligarch is not a self-made man. His family has been wealthy or siphoning money out of the public coffers or both for generations. He inherits a fleet of ships, invests minimally within Greece then blackmails whichever government happens to be in power, playing both ends of the political spectrum slyly and opportunistically. He is Western oriented. He is based in Athens or Piraeus or London or Zurich. He functions with the rest of the oligarchs as a class, strategically marrying his children off to other shipping and industrial families. He generally pieces together industries within Greece then divests his profits outside the country into a diversified mercantile empire spanning the Balkans and often stretching out to

eastern Europe and the Middle East.

Savvidis is something else – *to agnosto prosopo*, 'the unknown face'. A decade or so ago almost no one in Greece had heard his name. He owns no ships. He made his fortune outside of Greece and is now investing it within the country at an unthinkably inauspicious time. He is politically obtuse. He makes no attempt to ingratiate himself with – and, indeed, has provoked a feud with – the leadership of New Democracy, the party that was returned to power in 2019. Savvidis became the loyal instrument of the far-left Syriza government that climbed to power in 2015 on promises that it would rein in such figures but which instead gave them renewed licence to flourish. For the then prime minister, Alexis Tsipras, Savvidis was what's known as *imeteri*, 'one of our own', a figurehead of vast capital a government could use to outsource control of different sectors of the sprawling Greek state. In past interviews Savvidis compared Tsipras favourably with Putin and warned Tsipras's political adversary Kyriakos Mitsotakis, the leader of New Democracy and, as of 2019, prime minister of Greece, that he would never achieve that office. Curiously, Savvidis speaks only a mangled dialect of ancient Greek, which has curtailed his ability to address his ambitions in the Greek media. Savvidis has left it up to others to speculate what he is up to in Thessaloniki.

Critically, in a country whose oligarchic class has been unwaveringly loyal to

Euro-Atlanticism and US interests since the Second World War, Savvidis is an upstart from the East. His is a typically shadowy story of post-Soviet self-enrichment. He was born in 1959 into a large Greek peasant family in the mountains of southern Georgia. The history of his people, the Pontic Greeks, is one of generational displacement. The descendants of ancient Greek colonists of the Black Sea region, for centuries they lived on the northern cusp of Turkey as citizens of the Ottoman Empire. During the great population exchanges following the First World War most Pontic Greeks were forced to leave the new nation state of Turkey. Some 'returned' to Greece; others, like the Savvidis clan, migrated up the shores of the Black Sea and became citizens of another multinational empire, the Soviet Union. In the late 1930s Stalin sent hundreds of thousands of Pontic Greeks out to Central Asia, deeming them a fifth column of imperialism.

Savvidis belongs to those Pontic Greeks who never left the Black Sea. Historically bounded by empires, not unlike the Georgians and Armenians and Chechens in the mountains surrounding them, the Caucasus Greeks captured an economic niche through the cultivation of tobacco. At the age of fourteen Savvidis left their company, heading further up the shores of the Black Sea to Rostov-on-Don, where he rolled cigarettes on the floor of the Don State Tobacco Factory, took night classes at a local technical university, performed his military service and earned a reputation as a highly religious man. 'He had always attributed everything to God, ever since he was sleeping on his best man's couch in Rostov,' Sonia Prokopidi, a Pontic Greek who knew Savvidis before he came to Greece, told me in Thessaloniki. (In 2016 in Prochoma, a village along the Vardar River, Savvidis made a display of

GREEK SHIPOWNERS

Greece has the largest private merchant navy in the world, accounting for more than 15 per cent of the world's total tonnage (almost 40 per cent of that in the EU), including almost a quarter of the global fleet of oil tankers. The sector is estimated to be worth around 6 per cent of Greek GDP (a controversial figure, because the statistical agency ELSTAT considers the entire sector as if it were based in Greece, including dividends paid to non-Greek shareholders, for instance, or the wages of non-Greek sailors) and is said to provide employment to 4 per cent of the workforce (another disputed figure). There are over a thousand Greek shipowners with operations of all sizes, from the small (one or two ships) to the enormous: according to *VesselsValue*, the *Forbes* of the shipping world, John Angelicoussis, the largest Greek shipping magnate, had 129 ships in 2018, worth $7.6 billion (shipowners also have their version of Davos, the Posidonia shipping fair in Athens). A 1953 constitutional law has always guaranteed tax exemption on profits generated abroad, as well as a lower rate of VAT, but in 2019, for the first time, a Greek government was able to extract from the all-powerful Union of Greek Shipowners a promise to voluntarily pay 'at least' €75 million per year, the equivalent of 10 per cent of the union members' annual dividends. Over the years of the crisis the shipowners' fortunes have increased, along with orders for new ships (above all, in percentage terms, those designed to transport liquefied natural gas, LNG), thanks in part to significant Chinese investments.

his religious devotion. The fresco on the Church of the Holy Spirit depicts its benefactor in the supplicating kneeling position of a Byzantine saint, decked out in a black power suit, lifting a relic towards an enthroned Christ. He is flanked by his wife and two sons, all three of whom control various fiefs within his empire.)

With the collapse of the Soviet Union in 1991 Savvidis and hundreds of thousands of other Pontic Greeks embarked on a mass odyssey back to Greece, the first nation state they had known and yet a place that was effectively foreign to them. Known for harvesting tobacco in the USSR, in their ancestral homeland the Pontic Greeks gained a reputation for smuggling it in – first on fishing trawlers, later in cargo containers. It has never been clear to what extent Savvidis was involved in this trade, but by the time he returned to Russia just three years later he had emerged through the distant end of a murky acquisition scheme as the owner of Donskoy Tabak (the now-privatised Don State Tobacco Factory), then a middling cigarette company wrangling for control of the regional market. Rostov, the city to which Savvidis had returned, had become the proverbial 'father of mafias', an epicentre of post-Soviet turf wars, many waged over the very commodity routes – out west to the Donbas and lower Ukraine, down to the Caucasus, east to the Caspian Sea – that Savvidis would certainly have known well. A decade later, in 2003, he went to Moscow representing the Rostov Oblast in the Duma on Putin's United Russia ticket.

Savvidis spent the decade in between his return to Russia and his debut in the Duma collecting a diverse panoply of companies, including a sausage manufacturer, a dairy-packaging facility and a supplier of industrial-grade farm equipment. But his abiding preoccupation was always the

THE PISTOL-PACKING CHAIRMAN

It is hard to forget the episode that made Ivan Savvidis famous right across Europe and put him on the front page of numerous newspapers. It happened on Sunday 11 March 2018, during a football match between AEK and PAOK Thessaloniki. Savvidis, a Russian businessman with Greek roots, is chairman of the Thessaloniki club. Towards the end of the match the referee disallowed a PAOK goal, and Savvidis reacted by invading the pitch surrounded by his bodyguards – with a pistol clearly visible in the holster attached to his belt – and signalling to his players to leave the field. The atmosphere in the stadium was already boiling over, and violent disorder had broken out on the terraces, but the game was only abandoned for good when the police arrived.

THE PASSENGER   Alexander Clapp

A view of the port of Piraeus.

'In Greece, as in many countries, football crowds serve as extensions of political bases – a dangerous constituency for anyone in the press, the judiciary or the political arena to provoke.'

overhaul of Donskoy, turning it into the largest tobacco company in Russia. Some 30 billion cigarettes, or one in ten smoked in Russia, are produced by Donskoy annually, now under the formal management of Savvidis's wife Kyriaki, a fellow Pontic Greek. A special contract forged with the new Russian state – a deal in which to this day the Savvidis family hands out a billion free cigarettes to the Russian army every year – granted Donskoy an outsized role in crafting Russia's new tobacco legislation. On top of Donskoy, Savvidis acquired a handful of lesser assets, including an airport in Rostov and a fleet of Antonov cargo planes that pump cigarettes out across Central Asia and North Africa. Donskoy claims to send a disproportionate number of its 6 billion exported cigarettes to three outlaw statelets along the Black Sea – Transnistria, Abkhazia and South Ossetia – whose net populations amount to fewer than 800,000 people. Attributing profits to these unrecognised pseudo-states suggests either that Savvidis is earning his money by some other means – cigarette smuggling has been cautiously suggested in the Greek press – or is being funnelled in by an outside player. For the US and EU officials who have objected to his acquisition of the port of Thessaloniki, the suspected culprit is Vladimir Putin.

By the mid-2000s Savvidis had settled in Thessaloniki and, through a slew of Cypriot shell companies, begun his investments. He bought the PAOK football team, whose fan base has won him a maniacal personal following as well as a cheap form of insurance against significant investigations into his holdings. (In Greece, as in many countries, football crowds serve as extensions of political bases – a dangerous constituency for anyone in the press, the judiciary or the political arena to provoke.) Savvidis then moved on SEKAP, a deeply indebted state-owned tobacco producer in Thrace whose commercial networks throughout Greece and the eastern Mediterranean he has now integrated with the Black Sea networks commanded by Donskoy. (In June 2017 a fishing trawler manned by Ukrainians was seized off the coast of Crete en route from Montenegro, carrying millions of unregistered packets of Savvidis's Thracian tobacco to an unknown destination.) Next, Savvidis took over the Makedonia Pallas, a defunct former landmark hotel in northern Greece where he now regularly parks his black Mercedes. Eyebrows were then raised and the eye of the US State Department drawn during the complicated bidding process around the purchase of the port of Thessaloniki, an extraordinary strategic asset, because of the curious precision of Savvidis's bid, which managed just to edge out that put forward by the Dubai-based DP World.

The conduit between the crisis that first enriched Savvidis (the Soviet one) and the one through which he is currently divesting his wealth (the Greek one) is his ancient Pontic identity. He has become the figurehead for hundreds of thousands of Pontic Greeks who, to this day, have never felt properly assimilated into Greece. Savvidis himself has never learned the

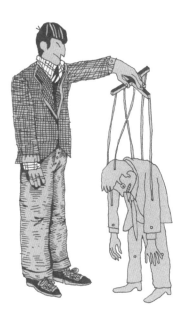

Diaploki (διαπλοκή)

The Greeks have managed to come up with a single word to describe the conflict of interests that typifies their country's political and administrative situation, thanks to the overlapping interests of politics, finance and business and media magnates – an almost incestuous relationship that goes against the public interest. *Diaploki* refers in particular to the vicious circle in which the media becomes a propaganda tool for governments, governments pass laws to distribute finance to the banks and the banks make loans to companies and political parties.

modern language. He fills his companies with Russians and Armenians, rarely Greeks. But he has suddenly, improbably, burst into the ranks of the Greek oligarchy. For these Greeks Savvidis is a hero. In May 2018 I watched as he inaugurated a new Pontic Greek studies department at Aristotle University in Thessaloniki. Hundreds of Pontic Greeks sat in attendance. They whipped out their camera phones en masse as Savvidis – a sturdy, bespectacled man with a trimmed grey beard and a compact gait – strutted on to a stage cluttered with priests and fuming with incense. Approaching the podium he nodded to a clutch of generals and Syriza ministers who had come up from Athens for the ceremony. Savvidis delivered his speech in Russian through a translator before attempting a short conclusion in Greek: 'For a long time we were ashamed to be Pontic Greeks. In this place we were considered foreigners. We were made to feel unwelcome,' he said. 'But you should never feel ashamed to be Pontic Greek again.' Loud applause followed.

'His story is my story,' a woman named Sultana whispered, turning to me. 'It's all our stories.'

This is Ivan Savvidis: a man who, through seemingly unlimited resources, has gained control of Greece's second city and won a fervent following among a potential voting bloc of some 400,000 Pontic Greeks – enough, perhaps, to sway a national election. If the allegations of Savvidis's connections to Putin are true, they would confirm in northern Greece what has previously been revealed in Serbia and Macedonia, namely that the Kremlin is using expatriate Russian oligarchs and their obscure financial networks to buy up state assets and undermine the decision-making of pro-European governments. That Putin himself has

Embarking for the islands from the port of Piraeus.

taken at least some interest in this venture became evident in May 2016, when he and Savvidis made a highly touted visit to St Panteleimon, a Russian monastic outpost on Mount Athos that has, in the last few years, been outfitted with five hundred new rooms and an assemblage of satellite systems.

But if Savvidis is emblematic of one type of oligarchic incursion into Greece – the kind acting on behalf of a foreign state – Victor Restis is something else. Not a vehicle of political interests but a transnational plunderer. Like Savvidis, he operates at the margins. Now in his early fifties, Restis is half a generation younger than the old oligarch guard, although his holdings are at least as extensive. His rise has been swift but circuitous, punctuated by scandal and shrouded in obscurity peculiar even by the standards of a Balkan billionaire.

Restis calls himself the new Aristotle Onassis but mostly shuns publicity. Shipping forms the backbone of his financial empire, but his real talent is for making forays into untapped corners of Europe, seizing assets, extracting connections and then heading off to pastures new. Restis's companies stretch across more than a dozen sectors – shipping, tourism, television, mining – and at least as many countries. Born in the Congo, educated in Belgium, in Athens he is an outsider, the Greek shipping magnate who does not descend from a Greek shipping dynasty. Restis's mother was born into a Jewish family from the island of Rhodes, the members of which were almost all exterminated at Auschwitz. His father, Stamatis, fled Greece soon after the end of its civil war in 1949 and, unlike most Greeks who headed to South Africa in the 1950s, made instead for the Congo. In Kinshasa Stamatis Restis built a modest fortune exporting fruits back to Europe. After Mobutu's nationalisation of

businesses in the late 1960s Stamatis left, returning to Piraeus and divesting his fruit earnings into a shipping company called Enterprises that was licensed two months before the collapse of the Colonels in 1974. Enterprises was a fleet of eighty-three vessels by the time a 36-year-old Victor took control following Stamatis's death in 2004.

Fifteen years later Restis remains better known outside of Greece than within it. 'He thrives on unpredictability,' I was told by his former business partner Anastasios Pallis. 'I know many shipowners. Restis does not work like any of them.' Whereas most oligarchs in Greece encircle themselves with a clutch of political worthies and shipping scions, surrounding Restis there is something else: a remarkable constellation of transnational opportunists and drifting profiteers whose interests bear, at first glance, no apparent reason for overlapping.

There is Milo Đukanović, the contraband cigarette baron who has lorded over Montenegro under one title or another since 1991. There is Thaksin Shinawatra, the ex-prime minister of Thailand, whose expansion of the electoral franchise (or rampant corruption, depending on your view) led to his 2006 ousting by his own army and who, three years later, re-emerged as the richest Montenegrin in the world, awarded citizenship of that country by Đukanović himself. There is Wei Seng 'Paul' Phua, the Malaysian card-sharp and serial match fixer who was taken down by an FBI sting operation in Las Vegas in 2014 only to resurface in the construction of Adriatic resort casinos in 2018. There is Claudio Podeschi, former head of the tiny mountain enclave of San Marino, indicted in 2015 on charges of hawking off diplomatic posts to, among others, Paul Phua – appointed San Marino's ambassador to Montenegro in early 2011 – as well as Victor

Restis, appointed San Marino's ambassador to Poland three months earlier. Working in collusion with each other, often taking cues from one another's schemes, these men have invested, reaped and transferred large sums of cash from one base of enrichment to the next. Restis is the figure most responsible for tying their operations together.

Victor Restis's story is worth considering for two reasons. The first is his personal demonstration of how, recurrently throughout the economic crisis, at a time when their financial arrangements have never appeared more indefensible, the most powerful men in Greece have brazenly violated its laws and walked away effectively unharmed. The second is that Restis's saga shows how easily such corruption can spread – especially in the wake of the Greek crisis, which encouraged the easy flow of dubious foreign capital into and through the country.

Restis's scandals within Greece are numerous. In 2013 his family bank, a sixteen-branch enterprise called First Business Bank, was shut down when he was accused of extracting loans from the state under the names of family members then siphoning the cash off to his offshore companies. Restis served four months of the five-year jail sentence, although he was acquitted in 2016.

At the same time allegations came from the US organisation United Against Nuclear Iran. Its claim was that Restis was the undisclosed owner of a ghost fleet – a collection of ships that unplug their GPS transmitters and cruise quietly in and out of harbours – that had been transporting from Iran to China crude oil worth hundreds of millions of euros bought with First Business Bank loans. Restis denied the accusation, fought it in a US court with a defamation lawsuit and came away claiming that his ships had merely been moving humanitarian aid – soya beans – through the Persian Gulf. (An intervention by the Obama administration in 2015 asserted that US intelligence sources, probably Israeli, would be exposed should all the relevant evidence have been brought out in court; Restis's suit was subsequently dismissed on national security grounds.) In 2018 legal scandal struck once more, with allegations that for at least five years Restis has been cleaning up his earnings through a storefront laundering racket in Athens that links out to an array of

THE MANY INTRIGUES OF VICTOR RESTIS

The rise of Victor Restis began after his father's death in 2004. He was an astute successor, immediately buying thirty-two cargo ships in Malaysia and becoming Greece's fifth largest shipowner, but, when the sector stalled shortly afterwards, he diversified his activities, moving beyond national boundaries. He acquired resorts in the Peloponnese and a football team in Glyfada; he bought castles in Umbria, built cruise ships in China and installed drilling rigs in the North Sea. He went on to bring MTV to the Balkans and bought news sites and shares in newspapers in Athens. He became a shareholder in banks based in Moldova, Romania and Turkey, while setting up the New Generation Bank in Germany. But his most significant presence is in Montenegro, where, since independence, the most

powerful political figure has been Milo
Đukanović. Restis arrived there when
his heavily indebted First Business
Bank was on the brink of seizure, and
the destinies of the two men became
intertwined. Restis also seems to
have links to the Thai consortium Pan
Asia Investments, which, in 2017,
began to speculate in Greece, buying
up hotel chains and attempting to
become a majority shareholder in
Panathinaikos, the country's oldest
football team. The consortium is
linked to the former Thai prime
minister, Thaksin Shinawatra. Restis
denies any involvement, although
Restis had replaced Shinawatra
on the board of Manchester City
Football Club in the English Premier
League in 2008. In December 2018
Restis received a ten-year prison
sentence for false declaration, but
this was suspended because his
lack of previous convictions.

offshore companies. His co-conspirator,
Ioannis Karouzos, is serving a sixteen-year
jail sentence. Restis appealed the verdict.

Which brings us to the second lesson of
the Restis affair, one that parallels the saga
of Ivan Savvidis, that the Greek crisis has
turned the country into an outsized repository for foreign capital flows – the result
of privatisations, a tourist industry whose
needs have doubled in the last decade and
the vast exodus of cash from Greek banks –
even while the provenances of that foreign
capital, and why it's coming to Greece, are
rarely apparent.

Ivan Savvidis, Victor Restis. One arrived
in Greece from Georgia, the other from the
Congo. One is based in Thessaloniki, the
other in Piraeus. But, for all their differences, these two men scheming on the margins speak a common truth about Greece
today. Their tactics are no less dirty than
those of the previous generation of Greek
oligarchs – men like Aristotle Onassis, the
magnate Restis publicly aspires to become,
who was a pioneer of global tax evasion.
But within the span of a few years, and
by European Union directive, the likes of
Savvidis and Restis have acquired what it
took the previous generation of oligarchs
decades to accumulate. And, under the
guise of performing a spring clean of the
Greek economy, Brussels will continue to
push the relentless privatisation of assets
that has afforded their ilk the cover for
quiet state capture.

The failure of one member of the EU to
rein in men such as this only leads to the
proliferation of their corruption everywhere: from Georgia to Russia to Greece;
from Montenegro to San Marino to Greece;
to wherever they set their sights next. In
the case of both men, one can already
imagine EU officials of the future puzzling
over the rotten state of Greece, wondering
how it could have ever happened again. ✒

A Way of Life

Rebetiko is rebel music – challenging power, war and conformism – part of the cultural baggage of those displaced from Asia Minor. In the past decade it has made a comeback and is once again showing its revolutionary potential.

MATTEO NUCCI
Translated by Alan Thawley

A concert by *rebetis* Thymios Stouraitis in a restaurant in the Exarchia district of Athens.

My initiation into rebetiko was by a Russian, Yianni, a skinny guy with a glassy look in his eyes softened by a glint of rebellion. He carries himself with self-respect and grace, and sooner or later you will come across him if you fall in love with this unique music and haunt the right places in Athens, the old-time venues, those that should never be named because they must stay on the fringes of the law. You will see him bent over his *tsipouro*, the Greek distilled spirit, his cigarettes rolled from the best tobacco. A blond dandy, a peaceful rebel. Yianni Litovchenko has a passion for this music. He smokes like a *rebetis*, a rebetiko musician, but he does not play and does not sing. He sits on the margins of these rooms full of music and ashtrays. And he listens. He dreams. Sometimes he will let out a yell or sing a verse under his breath. If you allow yourself to fall under the spell of this music, succumb to the tales he tells and follow him on his amazing night-time pilgrimages, the same thing that happened to me might also happen to you. At first I thought he was just someone rather unusual. I found out that he was born in Moscow but had been taken to America by his parents after just a few days in one of those Cold War escapes that made the news and which had condemned him to be forever stateless. His life before Athens was like something out of the movies. He had travelled the world throughout his teenage years, constantly on the move. Vising Greece in his twenties he had felt the spirit of certain ancestors on his mother's side still flowing through his veins and had decided to come back as soon as he could. Perhaps he had realised all this listening to rebetiko. Perhaps. Yianni says he is not sure. It is true that when rebetiko is worming its way under your skin you don't notice it, and only later do you realise you have caught the fever and you will never shake it off. I caught the rebetiko fever from Yianni, but I have no idea how long it has been running in his blood.

For me, it all began in earnest in around 2013. I always met Yianni in the same bar. We would chat a little, and, by some happy turn of events, he quickly realised what I needed, so one night he told me he would take me to hear Thymios play his bouzouki. I already knew quite a lot about rebetiko – I already knew the things that I'm telling you now – but I had not yet been enlightened. That happened that very evening when I felt something, a visceral sensation. As the old man Thymios Stouraitis played, with everyone around him quietly dreaming or crying or shouting, I felt the transfigurative spirit welling up inside me, that same

MATTEO NUCCI is a Roman author who has studied ancient philosophy and published essays on Empedocles, Socrates and Plato, editing and translating the latter's *Symposium* for the Italian publisher Einaudi. His first novel, *Sono comuni le cose degli amici* (Ponte alle Grazie, 2009), was shortlisted for the Premio Strega, as was *È giusto obbedire alla notte* (Ponte alle Grazie, 2017). More recent works include his essay *L'abisso di Eros* (Ponte alle Grazie, 2018). His articles and travel reportages are published in the weekly supplement of *La Repubblica, Il Venerdì*.

Dionysian spirit that Nietzsche attributed to Wagner and primordial music, a musical spirit that cannot truly be defined because it is a way of life, a way of seeing the world. These are things that have to blossom within before being put into words. Up to that point it had been a fleeting feeling that I had never been able to understand fully. I had done some research and was familiar with what you can find in any of the classic books on rebetiko. I knew it was a modal form of music with its roots lost in the oral traditions of the late nineteenth century. Even in the early days it was difficult to say what united these musicians of the most disparate origins beyond their subject matter – laments from the slums – a tendency to consume copious quantities of hashish (which was legal at the time) and playing certain Oriental-style instruments that would be abandoned when rebetiko became increasingly narrowly defined in the early years of the twentieth century. The key event was the Catastrophe of Smyrna, when more than 1.5 million Greeks from Asia Minor were forced to undertake an immense migration, an event I have discussed in relation to the routes taken by displaced people in ancient and modern times (see 'Lands of Migration' on page 33). The port city of Piraeus, which was already home to many *rebetes*, was flooded with men and women who had lost millennia of history. Life was hard on the streets, so hashish and the music of nostalgia and pride offered an escape route. A mixture of traditions representing the refined music of Smyrna marked the beginning of the golden age of rebetiko.

Those who are unable to explain this music call it the 'Greek blues', but really there is no definition. What happens in every book on this music of life and death is truly symptomatic: after listing a series of possible definitions, the authors give up

MISIRLOU

She is an Egyptian girl with honeyed lips, an exotic, black-eyed beauty who has stolen the hearts of singers all over the world for over a century. She is Misirlou, the subject of a traditional Greek song recorded for the first time in 1927, in the rebetiko style, by Tetos Dimitriadis, a Greek born in Istanbul who had recently emigrated to the USA. In 1941 the Greek jazz musician Nick Roubanis released an instrumental version, crediting himself as the writer (and, seeing as no one took the trouble to contradict him, it is still legally attributed to him). The song became a sensation in the Mediterranean, with versions in Arabic and Yiddish, and every country where an Egyptian girl has ever set foot laid claim to it. In 1963 it was the turn of Richard Mansour, the son of a Lebanese immigrant, who performed under the name of Dick Dale and was a pioneer of surf rock. Legend has it that during a concert the audience asked him to play something using just one string of his guitar. He remembered 'Misirlou', a song he used to hear as a child, and played it at twice the speed. Global success came over thirty years later when the movie director Quentin Tarantino used the song as the title track of *Pulp Fiction*, ensuring Dick Dale – and the Egyptian girl – would become immortal in Hollywood (Dick Dale died in March 2019). There was still time for the song to come home, however, when the Greek singer Anna Vissi performed a pop version in a storm of blue and white confetti at the closing ceremony of the 2004 Olympics.

A rebetiko performance
by Thymios Stouraitis
in a restaurant
in the Exarchia district
of Athens.

'Rebetes lived from day to day, walking the streets in search of friends and love or a place to play and sing of their pain and their dreams.'

and move on to something else. They try to get to the heart of the matter through tangential descriptions then conclude with a final section in which a selection of songs is reproduced with commentaries and translations. Because the soul of rebetiko and the soul of the *rebetis* (plural *rebetes*) cannot be pinned down. The same is true of the soul of the *mangas* (plural *manges*). Ask a few Greeks, and each time you will be given a different definition of these key terms. Elias Petropoulos, the first writer to publish an extensive study of rebetiko (1968), does come to some conclusions. Petropoulos was an author, anthropologist and student of Greek language and customs, but above all a philosopher of the underground who spent long stretches in prison because of his libertarian opinions. He found it hard to believe that the word *rebetis*, of Turkish origin, was not connected to the term used by the Venetians to define a spirit of rebellion (*rebelos*). The *rebetes* came from the slums. They were marginalised outcasts, opponents of the bourgeois spirit in a metahistorical sense, an embodiment of defiance in the face of established power but also in the face of death, the highest power of all. The *manges*, on the other hand, were the dominant, dandy-like figures in a neighbourhood, handing out money with disdain (for the money) and cultivating a reserved, aloof attitude. Men (and women, too, because women are not relegated to supporting roles in this story) who ruled over the streets with pride, showed stoic resistance to the agonies of the soul, have a propensity to enjoy life and a dignity that

they would defend with any weapon. The *rebetes*' only weapon was the pear-shaped mandolin known as the bouzouki and the *baglamas*, the miniature version that came into fashion when the instrument was banned by the authorities; *manges*, however, were often armed with knives as well. All true *rebetes* were *manges*, but not all *manges* were *rebetes* – you could put it like that, but nothing is certain. Perhaps there is only one way to separate the two, as Gail Holst states in that other classic volume on rebetiko, *Road to Rembetika*: *rebetes* and *manges* are the same but different. There you have it. In any case, to those observing from a distance the most important thing is the common element, which lay to a large extent in a quality of the soul, in their bravado, their romantic attachment to a lost homeland and the waking dream of recreating this homeland within themselves. A homeland built on candour, simplicity and a desire to live each day to the full without making plans and free from the dominion of time as a linear process. *Rebetes* lived from day to day, walking the streets in search of friends and love or a place to play and sing of their pain and their dreams. In the beginning these places were bare-walled rooms called *tekedes* (singular *tekes*), anonymous venues that opened up in the largest of the single-storey shacks that had sprung up on the shores of the Saronic Gulf, off the coast of Athens and Piraeus, and around the port of Thessaloniki. Very basic dictionaries will tell you that the *tekedes* were hash dens. This is partly true. Protected from the dazzling sun of summer and the cold of winter, patrons of the *tekedes* would smoke hookahs packed with hashish to lose the sense of their own individuality in the sublime state of *mastoura*. But, as well as smoking water pipes, people played and sang to delicate, unending rhythms until night fell and the notion of time dissipated. Men and women would come and go, then some would start their hypnotic, solitary dances, and finally every man and woman was simply part of a single animal existence, uniting everyone without distinction.

When Yianni and I entered the magnificent neoclassical house that a fisherman had decked out as a release for his rebetiko passions, I had the sensation that this was finally the *tekes* I had always been looking for. Of course, we can only dream of the rough-and-ready atmosphere that must have dominated in those first glorious years, during the so-called Piraeus era of the 1920s (reconstructions of which can be seen in the marvellous sets in Kostas Ferris's film *Rembetiko*, which won the Silver Bear in Berlin in 1984). But in the large room in the neoclassical building where Yianni took me that sweltering June night there was still a certain rawness in the air, that rough surface that is the skin of rebetiko. The bare walls, the lighting low but not cloying, the smoke-filled air, the unmistakeable smell of hashish and marijuana, a thick and tremulous silence in the air vibrating to Thymios Stouraitis's bouzouki and his husky voice. His partner Maria sang along, standing erect, a stern look in her eyes, as Thymios became one with his instrument, holding a cigarette in the *rebetis* way between the little finger and the ring finger of his right hand as it danced over the metal strings. We had entered a different world and been welcomed into a different space–time configuration a few metres away from the noise of the hipster bars. The established laws did not apply. They came in droves, young and old, girls and boys. It was four in the morning, and the place was packed to the rafters, the windows open on to the dark surrounding streets, as Thymios carried on playing. At around 5 a.m. he began to really let loose, launching into versions of classic songs that shook you to the core. We left as day was breaking, and Thymios was still going, even though the room was almost empty by then.

Out on the street Yianni explained why this musician approaching his eighties, whom he called 'the old man', was, in his opinion, the last true *rebetis*, the last true *mangas*. 'When you ask other musicians if they have the same lifestyle as in days gone by, they all say yes, they're *rebetes*, they're *manges*. Then you ask him, and he says, "Me, a *mangas*? What are you on about?" This humility already counts in his favour, but then, if you follow him, you realise he's the only one who still lives that way of life to the full.' Because Thymios Stouraitis leads a timeless existence. He has no bank account. He lives on what little he earns from his performances. His house is very simple, a little cement cube outside of Athens in a suburb called Keratea, right in the middle of Attica in a landscape dominated by rocks, dust and olive trees. Following a nomadic youth, he has lived here with Maria for twenty-five years and now spends his life in a constant search for inner peace divorced from the rhetoric that sees evil in war. Polemos, an ancient Greek personification of war, is the father of all, said Heraclitus. The *rebetes* know there is no music without crisis, no peace without war, so alongside the countless songs about hashish (known as *chasiklidika*), there are compositions about prison and the underworld, tavernas and love, work and family, nostalgia and death. At the heart of everything is an attitude: the sense of pride

Rebetiko in eleven steps

1
Markos
Vamvakaris
'Frangosyriani'

2
Sotiria Bellou
'Mi mou
xanafygeis pia'

3
Michalis
Patrinos
'Misirlou'

4
Marika Papagika
'Manaki mou'

5
Giannis Dragatsis
'Manolis o chassiklis'

6
Kostas Bezos
'Paximadokleftra'

7
Vassilis Tsitsanis
'Synnefiasmeni
Kyriaki'

8
Markos Vamvakaris
'Ta matoklada sou
lamboun'

9
Estoudiantina
tis Neas Ionias
'Den se thelo pia'

10
Rosa Eskenazi
'Giati foumaro
kokaini'

11
Kostas
Skarvelis
'Ematha pos
isse mangas'

Listen to this playlist at:
open.spotify.com/user/iperborea

Rebetiko in its own words

Marika Papagika
Manaki mou ('My Baby')

Baby child, baby child
My poor head is all riled
Baby child, oh my, oh my
No finer man ever you'll find
Why are you looking at me like that
Thought I'd be scared of you, I bet?
That place where you go, that
place where you go,
You are to go to that place no more
Go there no more and you'll be fine
Or else your neck is on the line
My cloak's gone missing somewhere
And all because I took no care
Sir, policeman, sir, stop beating me
Poor soul that I am, this wasn't my doing

Markos Vamvakaris
Ta matoklada sou lamboun
('Your Eyelashes Shine')

Your eyelashes shine
Like the flowers of the prairie
Like the flowers of the prairie
Your eyelashes shine

Sister, your sweet eyes
They break my heart
They break my heart
Your sweet eyes, sister

You lower your lashes
And I am left with no words or sense
I am left with no words or sense
You lower your lashes

No matter how hard you search
You'll not find another like me
You'll not find another like me
No matter how hard you search

Marika Papagika
Ti se meli esenane ('What's It to You?')

What's it to you
From where I hail
If it's Kardassi or Kordelio,
Light of my eyes?

What's it to you
That you keep asking
Which village I am from
If you don't love me?

Where I am from
People know how to love
They know how to hide their pain
They know how to rejoice

What's it to you
That you keep asking
If you can't pity me, light of my eyes,
And only toy with me?

It is from Smyrna that I come
Looking for balm
In our Athens, looking to find
A pair of loving arms

Traditional
Misirlou

My Misirlou, your sweet eyes
Have lit a flame in my heart
Ah ya habibi, ah ya leleli, ah
Honey drips from your lips

Ah, Misirlou, your magical exotic beauty
Will drive me crazy
I can't stand it any more
Ah, I will steal you from Arabia

My black-eyed Misirlou
My life changes with a kiss
Ah ya habibi, with a little kiss, ah
From that little mouth of yours, ah!

and dignity, steadfastness in finding your own way outside the idiocies that govern the world of appearances, the unquenchable thirst for justice.

It was an epiphany that pushed Thymios towards rebetiko. As a child he went from village to village playing a mandolin with his violinist father. Then he heard Markos Vamvakaris play during a triumphant appearance in one of these run-down little places, and everything changed. These days you don't need to mention his surname: Markos is regarded as the true soul of golden-age rebetiko. And what happened to Thymios was the exact same thing that had happened to Markos. Markos was born on Syros, the Catholic island in the Cyclades, and arrived in Piraeus before the Catastrophe of Smyrna. In Piraeus, while working at the slaughterhouse, he heard the bouzouki playing of Nikos Avaliotis, who, after ten years in prison, played Eastern-inflected melodies like a god. Markos listened to his songs of incarceration and hashish, and six months later it was his turn to impress the old man. He had learned everything; he was ready to play in the *tekedes* to the dreaming *manges* sitting with their backs against the walls, borsalino hats down over their eyes and hookahs in their mouths, feeding hashish into their brains. Vamvakaris, with his rough, stark voice, was responsible for the first recordings that in the 1920s enabled record labels to push rebetiko beyond its oral traditions. Markos, the writer of future classics, was also the musician who found himself at the crossroads between the traditions of Piraeus and those of the people who arrived in Piraeus from Smyrna following the Catastrophe. Elias Petropoulos believes there have been three key periods in the history of rebetiko: the first (1922–32) was dominated by the Smyrna style grafting on to the Piraeus

tradition; the second (1932–40) was marked by growing public success that led to the 'bourgeois' reaction, the bans imposed by the Metaxas dictatorship (which held power from 1936) and musicians being sent to prison; the third (1940–52) was the era of war, hunger, terror and the re-emergence from those tragedies with the smoother, more popular songs of Vassilis Tsitsanis. Later, rebetiko exhausted its vital drive, and the repertoire became restricted to songs that had already been written; these songs were the classics, and any musician arriving on the scene has to engage with them, playing and reinterpreting them rather than writing original music.

So is it a dead musical form, one without a future? This was playing insistently on my mind as I walked through the streets of Metaxourgio one evening. I found myself following the music into another sort of clandestine *tekes*, without Yianni or Thymios but surrounded by a throng of teenagers, their eyes clouded by hashish, fervently singing songs written almost a century before they were born. The answer was obviously no. I think anyone who loves this music and follows its strange vitality could confirm this. Many things have happened in recent years, and not just changes in the forms of rebetiko. Some young rebels have even started to write their own material – although it is difficult to imagine a future for any song that people can't just start singing in a café, one that has not been in the blood since birth. But that is not the point. It is the *spirit* of rebetiko that has burst back on to the scene, the soul of the *rebetes*, their way of life. With the financial crisis, upheaval in traditions and customs, poverty, repossessions, rapacious banks, lethal debts, clashes with the forces of law and order, the revolution always around the corner, the idea of Europe to fight over, closed-down businesses, unemployment,

> 'With the crisis, upheaval in traditions and customs, poverty, repossessions, rapacious banks, lethal debts, the wars on the street, the lack of health cover, rebetiko has once again become a strong, clear response.'

lack of health cover, taxes like guillotines and a pervasive sense of a genuine crisis, rebetiko has once again become a powerful response, a certainty full of doubt to rally around, an island of authenticity and pride, a refuge of tranquillity in the constant search for new paths. Back to the land, back to the homeland, to what we love, to what they want to take from us. But how? What weapons are they going to use to take it from us? Today the answer is clearer than ever with the numbing of tastes, globalisation, homogenisation, the imposition of consumerism and typically Protestant hyper-productivity. But we must resist, rebel, puff out our chests and ignore the insults, bear the pain and defy death. We must get back to simplicity, to liberation from the unnecessary and superfluous desires, seek out only what can help us to live well, become *meraklis*, wedded to our own passions, enjoying time and the things that we truly love, doing what we do with all of our love.

Rebetiko is a way of life not a way of thinking or simply a way of making music. This is what Elias Petropoulos wrote. This is what Yianni continues to say. Courage and generosity, shunning the rules of economic profit in a spiritual as well as in a material sense. I follow behind him as he walks down the street pursuing an idea. 'Perhaps it's too late, Yianni,' I tell him, and he replies, 'Oh Matteo, it's always too late for people like us.' And so I follow him. I know he will find a place where we can sit and immerse ourselves in the music, a place to lose our own sense of individuality, as Nietzsche said. To feel like humans, all belonging to the same animal kingdom. The Dionysian. The orgiastic intoxication of song that unites us all outside of the trappings that conventional lives have tried to impose upon us. And, as I follow him through the dark alleys of Athens and the underground walkways where you find famous tavernas and the tumbledown buildings that conceal the treasures within, I am reminded of one of the most extreme *rebetes* of the twentieth century, a minor, almost forgotten figure, Vangelis Papazoglou. In 1937 Metaxas's censors asked him to rework one of his lyrics: 'I am desperately searching for my fate to ask her if I have the right to live in freedom.' Replace 'freedom' with 'happiness', they told him, or be censored. But Papazoglou refused. 'Only those who can be free are happy,' he replied. From that day on he stopped writing songs. And when the Germans occupied Athens he stopped singing as well. 'The birds don't sing when it gets dark,' he would say. He was right, but only partly so. Dawn is breaking on the streets of Athens. You can already feel the approach of spring. 🐦

A rebetiko performance at a venue in the Metaxourgio district of Athens.

An Overdose of Love

New Greek cinema has been the country's
leading cultural export in recent years.
This new wave that international critics
are determined to label 'crisis cinema'
has been celebrated abroad, but its
destabilising success has left the Greeks
themselves perplexed. They have seen
Yorgos Lanthimos, its leading light,
leave to work in London and want to
see a little more love for their country.

DIMITRIS PAPANIKOLAOU
Translated by Konstantine Matsoukas

A vintage projector
at the Trianon cinema,
Athens.

The week before the ninety-first Oscars ceremony, at which Yorgos Lanthimos's international co-production *The Favourite* was nominated for ten awards, the Greek Association of Film Producers-Directors put out a video to wish him luck. The video, *Letters to Yorgos Lanthimos*, was shot in the seaside town of Kineta, the location in which Lanthimos himself had, in 2005, filmed his own first experimental movie. Seen on a bus and then wandering around empty hotels, beaches and streets, the actor Makis Papadimitriou, known for his roles in a run of recent Greek movies, reads out a letter to the best-known Greek director of the day:

'Dear Yorgos, there are no words to describe the national pride we all feel right now. We are counting and re-counting the Oscar nominations and cheering you on. Still, I did expect this because I have always believed in you and in Greek cinema. You may now be walking around Santa Monica surrounded by dazzling stars and unrelenting paparazzi, but I always remember that things had their beginnings on another more humble beach. A beach by the name of Kineta. Above all else, Greek cinema requires love. You, Yorgos, know this better than anyone. And, for sure, while you're making Greek cinema proud the world over, we remember all the things that are keeping you away from us.'

At this point banners cross the screen listing reasons that would make a Greek director disillusioned with the state of Greek cinema: 'lack of strategy, lack of coordination, lack of funding, ineffective institutions, inertia of the Ministry of Culture, indifference of the state'. The video concludes with a slogan aimed at all those institutions and also the viewers (if not also to the directors themselves): 'Give Greek cinema a little love'.

The video brings together some of the characteristics of recent Greek filmmaking, which, certainly since 2009 (that is, the years the Greek and international media refer to as the 'Greek crisis'):

· has continued to make films that are nominated for and frequently win awards at international festivals;

· has given birth to a new generation of filmmakers considered by Greek and international public opinion to be a clearly defined group (although this may not actually be the case);

· has set a benchmark – that is, one recognises it as 'new' filmmaking with milestone films: *Dogtooth* (2009); *Strella* (a.k.a. *A Woman's Way*; 2009); *Plato's Academy* (2009); *Attenberg* (2010); *Homeland* (2010); *Alps* (2011); *Boy Eating the Bird's Food* (2012); *Miss Violence* (2013);

· employs actors widely recognised in Greece and, occasionally, internationally;

· has continued to face a series of

DIMITRIS PAPANIKOLAOU is an associate professor of Modern Greek at Oxford University. In Greece he is very well-known for his articles on politics and culture for various national newspapers. He has also written three monographs, and his upcoming publications include *Greek Weird Wave: A Cinema of Biopolitics* for Edinburgh University Press.

'The invitation to "give Greek cinema a little love" is not addressed just to the chronically underfunded filmmaking agencies, it is aimed squarely at the Greek public, too.'

problems including, among others, a lack of institutional support and funding.

The video refers to two more elements that one perhaps needs a bit of local knowledge to spot. The first is the gap between the international recognition that Greek cinema has received (to the point of taking Hollywood by storm through the work of Lanthimos) and the comparatively low public appeal of these movies in Greece, where they are referred to either as Weird Wave or New Wave. The invitation to 'give Greek cinema a little love' is not addressed just to the chronically underfunded film-making agencies, it is aimed squarely at the Greek public, too, which doesn't appear to have embraced Greece's internationally best-known product of the crisis years: its cinema.

Second, the jocular tone of the video appears to be something of an in-joke, one for filmmakers, because it makes direct reference to the style and setting of several well-known Greek films of recent times. Kineta, the area through which Makis Papadimitriou wanders while reading his letter to Lanthimos, is a middle-class tourist resort a short distance from Athens, characterised, if not by abandonment then by funding cuts and neglect in the wake of overdevelopment. Filming someone walking through the empty streets of Kineta, particularly in winter, in front of the desolate concrete houses and along the cracked pavements, the backdrop itself is suddenly imbued with a sense of allegory – a national allegory. Add one or two off-beat elements: people wearing mismatched clothing, slowing the film down and using odd camera angles that produce chopped-up or overturned bodies. Weird scenery, weird conversation, weirdly filmed. Even without wanting to, you start to understand what you are watching metaphorically, allegorically. You see the abandoned semi-urban landscape and think of the country; you see the frame jammed and you think of a country in crisis.

The story I want to tell goes by the name of Greek Weird Wave, Greek New Wave or Greek crisis cinema, and it all began a few years ago. It is worth starting from the beginning.

*

Yannis Economides's film *Matchbox* was made in 2001, was first presented at festivals in 2002 and came out in Greek cinemas, after some delay, in 2003 without becoming a major box-office success. However, it has over time become legendary, and there's hardly a Greek not familiar with at least some of its scenes – which is down to the film's later widespread availability on DVD, on the internet, in theatrical adaptations but also simply as a point of reference: the word 'matchbox' has become synonymous with a peculiarly Greek outbreak of family tension and, for some, a synonym for the new Greek cinema.

I don't know if the movie was what is called far ahead of its time, but it certainly came at a time when a great many people didn't quite get what it was trying to convey, what its point was. 'I remember watching the film at a festival,' a critic told me, 'and only a few people stayed to the end, a few Greek critics and some

THE PASSENGER   Dimitris Papanikolaou

An Overdose of Love

Pages 160–1: An audience
watching a documentary
at the Trianon cinema (left);
a bust of Andrei Tarkovsky
in the reception area of the
Greek Film Archive, Athens
(right).

foreigners who kept asking us if all Greek families were like the one portrayed. It was very hard for them to take in a movie in which nothing happens apart from yelling, bullying, cursing, outrageous language and scenes between the family members.' Indeed, it is very difficult, even today, to watch *Matchbox* without having an intense reaction. In the film, a middle-class family devours itself for eighty minutes, without a break, without any let-up, without even opening a door for some air to come into its closed-off, nouveau-riche home.

In Greece at the time everyone was, of course, talking about the 'marvel of the Olympics' that were coming and was complacently fixated on what the country would be showcasing during the games – even if what the country actually showed the world that summer was somewhat haphazard and makeshift. (As haphazard and makeshift as the tree planting in Athens in that summer of 2004 – a few months later most of the trees and plants that had been verdant in August were already dried up; and after a few years the sports facilities themselves stood neglected – the ideal setting for films that deal with social exclusion, marginalised youth and national decline, such as Sofia Exarchou's 2016 *Park*.)

At the beginning of the new century's first decade, however, the country certainly seemed to be prospering and, an important point, to be united in a spirit of national confidence that it hadn't experienced for many years and which was celebrated with the flying of flags and people out on the streets of the large cities on any and every occasion: the completely unexpected win in the finals of the UEFA European Football Championship in 2004, all the highlights of the 2004 Olympics, even Elena Paparizou's victory in the Eurovision Song Contest in 2005. With a nation in such high spirits there wasn't much room for a film taking place inside four walls, portraying a Greek family far removed from the stereotype of the 'holy Greek family' that many would like to promote as representative of the country; this is a family in a state of panic, constantly at war with itself, showing off its newly acquired material wealth. This did not chime with the image of Greece and Hellenism being actively pushed at the time.

Some, a few perhaps, might consider the neurotic family in *Matchbox* and the mutual carnage of its members to be realistic (besides, neuroses have traditionally abounded behind the closed doors of Greek homes), but even they would agree that it might not be appropriate for this image to be promoted further afield. It is certain, however, that at that point no one was in a position to see in this image of a deep, persistent and painful inner crisis an allegory of an entire country.

A few years later, after December 2008, quite a few people would call that film to mind. Suddenly, occasioned by the murder in Exarchia in the centre of Athens of fifteen-year-old Alexandros Grigoropoulos by an on-duty policeman, the 'country on the rebound' with its beautiful bodies (on the sports field, in the museum or on the beach) turned into a country of chaos, with young people taking to the streets in protest, demanding to be heard, calling

'No one was in a position to see in this image of a deep, persistent and painful inner crisis an allegory of an entire country.'

for strikes, denouncing the entire social structure as corrupt. And the country that up until then had been seen as the birthplace of the Olympic flame became, all of a sudden, a country in flames, burning out of control. December 2008 saw the torching of the Christmas tree in Syntagma Square (along with buildings in the vicinity) being broadcast internationally. These images of extreme unrest in Athens would be repeated often in the years to come.

After December 2008 everything in Greece was being contested, and the international economic crisis, slowly and inexorably becoming a Greek national crisis, appeared, paradoxically, to support this mood of confrontation. In this atmosphere a new generation of Greek filmmakers decided to enter the fray, considering that the traditional system of production and support for Greek cinema was already outdated and certainly part of the problem rather than the basis for any kind of solution. They called themselves 'Filmmakers in the Fog', or FOG (FOG being an acronym for Filmmakers of Greece but also a reference to a 1988 film by Theodoros Angelopoulos, *Landscape in the Mist*). As a group, FOG aimed to declare their intention to pursue a new wave of Greek cinema.

Coincidentally or not, two films that appeared almost simultaneously in Greek cinemas in the winter of 2009 were linked to this new movement and seemed to pick up where *Matchbox* had left off. *Strella*, by Panos Koutras, is the story of a trans sex-worker and an impossible, traumatic love affair with an older man who turns out to be her father; *Dogtooth*, by Yorgos

Lanthimos, is the tale of a five-member family who live closed off in a comfortable suburban home under absolute paternal rule, with the children never having seen the world beyond the walls of their garden and submitting to the patriarch's biopolitical power without protest while harbouring the occasional thought that they might at some point get away. These two films are completely different in form and material, in their creators themselves, yet both returned to the theme of the family – presenting, once again, hidden traumas *inside* the family home but also the family members' attempts, against all the odds, to extricate themselves from this familial cage. Both films, after their auspicious tours of international festivals, secured widespread distribution internationally – something that hadn't happened to Greek cinema for years. They sparked a dialogue.

In those same months Greece was entering what eventually became known as the Greek crisis, the fallout from the international economic situation that plunged the country into a debt crisis and one of the most dramatic falls in standards of living – alongside the decimation of wages and pensions with a concurrent rise in taxes and unemployment – experienced anywhere in post-war Europe.

During the winter of 2009–10 Greeks were hearing about economic quotas of failure, thresholds that had been exceeded, European partners pressing for radical solutions and a society in turmoil. The two best-known films showing in Greek cinemas during those months were about families on the point of meltdown; at that

The Greek director Theo Angelopoulos occupies a special place among the great names of auteur cinema. He is also known outside of Greece thanks to collaborations with great actors such as Marcello Mastroianni and Jeanne Moreau, and his monumental body of work has earned him countless awards. In his films, with their dream-like atmospheres, he poetically reveals existential dramas and traumatic episodes of Greek history, portraying a nation torn between an invented tradition of past glories and a traumatic history of dictatorships and corrupt politics. In *The Travelling Players* (1975), for instance, we follow the adventures of a theatrical troupe during the Second World War, the fall of Metaxas and the election of Marshal Papagos. Angelopoulos's films reveal the sense of disorientation in Greece caused by the tension between present and past, but together they re-establish the ancient greatness of epic stories with the sweeping rhythm of grand narratives such as *Eternity and a Day* (1998) and *Alexander the Great* (1980). Another recurring theme is that

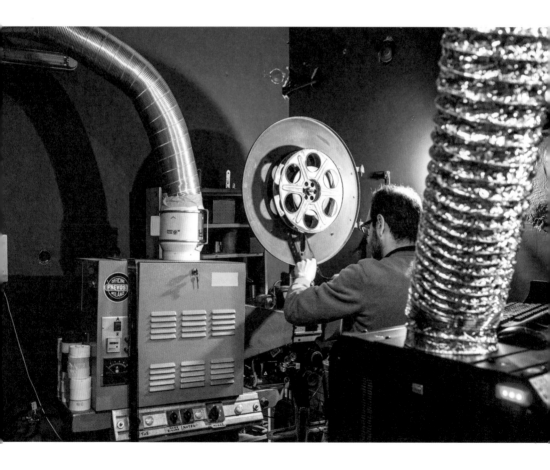

of a sense of incompleteness: a journey that does not reach its destination, stories without endings, but also the awareness that everything is part of life's mystery. The two children in *Landscape in the Mist* (1988) want to get to Germany to find their father but cannot; Spiros in *The Beekeeper* (1986) decides on a new career and sets off from northern Greece to the wildest corner of the south without knowing what he is looking for. And yet his films transcend personal tragedy and are able to delicately convey the universal through fragments of the everyday.

A projectionist at the Trianon cinema loads a reel into a vintage projector that is still in regular use.

same time the prime minister, George Papandreou, and Greece's 'European partners' were talking about the need to save them all, together, like one big family.

Describing the situation in such terms, Papandreou appeared on 23 October 2010 at the far-flung island of Kastellorizo and publicly declared that he would seek recourse to the support mechanisms of the European Union and the International Monetary Fund 'in order to set Greece back on its feet' and so that it might find 'a safe harbour'. I know several people who, listening to that speech, thought that he spoke like a father; that the tiny port of Kastellorizo where he delivered his address seemed enclosed all around, woefully

closed in, as if to symbolise that there was no escape, although the picturesque houses and blue waters were also intended to signify that all would be well. I have no idea how many, but I know that some who saw George Papandreou that morning in Kastellorizo thought: *Dogtooth*.

On 10 May 2010, at the Athens Concert Hall, the first awards of the Greek Cinema Academy – the newly established institution the Filmmakers in the Fog had founded in order to show their independence and distance from Greek cinema's previous centres of production, distribution and recognition – were presented. The top awards went, predictably, to *Dogtooth* and *Strella*. On that same morning of 10 May Greece submitted its application to come under the financial support mechanism, embarking on the series of rescue programmes and extreme austerity measures that came to be known as 'memoranda'. No matter if no one had intended it, even if it were just a series of coincidences, these films, *Dogtooth* and *Strella*, but also the whole New Wave of which they now appeared to be the successful forerunners, were inextricably linked with the Greek crisis. If not, at least for now, in the minds of Greek viewers (who had other, more pressing matters to attend to just then), certainly in the minds of the international media, which seemed to be anxiously searching for a symbolic image to illustrate what was happening. The main publicity shot from *Dogtooth*, of incarcerated children lined up in a festively decorated milieu, and with something about the whole scene seeming both familiar and paradoxical, remained for years the illustration accompanying all kinds of writings about Greece and the crisis. Even if the Greek family as portrayed in these movies, this 'family in meltdown', hadn't been produced as a commentary on the particular financial and socio-political development in the country, the theme became inextricably linked with it.

Is the family the 'root of all of evil' in Greek society? Is it a 'machine that perpetrates rage, which grows from one generation to the next'? Greek reporters and critics asked such questions, as information on films about the family in meltdown (not to mention similarly themed plays, art exhibitions, novels and poetry collections) kept popping into their inboxes. Seeing such material, Steve Rose, a critic for the *Guardian*, concluded an article, '*Attenberg*, *Dogtooth* and the Weird Wave of Greek Cinema', by asking whether it was just a coincidence that the world's most messed-up country was making the world's most messed-up cinema.

In the years that followed, supported by this international interest and also, probably, attempting to engage with the expectations implicit therein, Greek cinema produced some of its more widely discussed and award-winning films. A circle centred on directors Yorgos Lanthimos and Athina Rachel Tsangari and scriptwriter Efthimis Filippou created movies with international appeal: *Dogtooth*, *Attenberg*, *Alps*, *Chevalier*, *The Lobster*, *The Killing of a Sacred Deer*. In all of them irony prevails, there are empty spaces (often urban), paradoxical or absurdist moments in the plot, scenes of sudden violence and a predilection for visual allegory that combine with the actors' emotional distance in the delivery of their lines, an emphasis on the control of bodies and minds (hence the many scenes of education or hospitalisation) and the use of unusual camera angles. When foreign critics reference Weird Greek Cinema, these are the principal elements they have in mind.

Not all Greek movies of the past fifteen years have been in this vein. After *Matchbox* Yannis Economides continued creating films featuring violence in enclosed spaces and intimate family and social relationships (*Soul Kicking*, *Cutthroat*, *The Little Fish*). Panos Koutras complemented *Strella* with *Xenia*, another queer movie about Greek society and the concept of citizenship. Syllas Tzoumerkas, Filippos Tsitos, Konstantina Voulgari, Thanos Anastasopoulos, Hector Lygizos and Yannis Sakaridis turned rather to an inventive social realism and a more linear filming of the crisis years, often with an emphasis on the subcultures that emerged, especially in the large cities. Elina Psykou, Alexis Alexiou, Angelos Frantzis, Alexandros Voulgaris and Yannis Veslemes explored (often with an allegorical intention) the limits of the cinematic genre.

Were all these films about the family? Certainly not, yet the wider network of kinship, gender and sexuality as well as personal relationships were often their subjects, with a particular emphasis on the power and control that enter into these aspects of human life.

Were all these films about the crisis – or, at least, did they relate to it? One could say no – besides, more often than not, Greek films do not refer directly to the social conditions in Greece today. Yet that context ended up, often indirectly, bound up with the films; it ended up, that is, being a part of the way these films were viewed by international festivals and their audiences and eventually by audiences in Greece.

And should all these films come under the heading Weird Wave, a messed-up cinema from the world's most messed-up country? Many Greek directors and critics have argued for the non-literal interpretation of this. What exactly does 'weird' mean anyway, apart from one's inability to understand (or indifference to) why something is happening? Yet the term stuck, as any internet search will show. Under

Essential Viewing

Michael Cacoyannis
STELLA
1955

A realist reconstruction of post-war Athens, this is the story of an explosive love affair, gender subordination and insubordination and popular culture. Strong, proud women and vulnerable men, visions of Greek tavernas and impoverished neighbourhoods, as well as probably Melina Mercouri's finest role. From the director who went on to give us *Electra* (1962) and *Zorba the Greek* (1964).

Theo Angelopoulos
THE TRAVELLING PLAYERS
1975

The greatest Greek film of last century, a classic of world cinema and an inspiration for many directors (including Bernardo Bertolucci for *1900*). We view the history of twentieth-century Greece through the travels of a theatrical family, whose names are taken from Aeschylus' *Oresteia* and who journey back and forth in various different eras through rural Greece. The dramatic moments are approached as acts in a cyclical and never-ending tragedy.

Athina Rachel Tsangari
ATTENBERG
2010

In an underpopulated town, two young women discover sexuality, relationships, the urban landscape and friendship, turning them all on their heads. Filmed in the industrial, modernist city of Aspra Spitia, this is a feminist coming-of-age story that also works as an allegory of Greece's lost modernisation. Athina Rachel Tsangari also produced *Alps* (2011) and *Dogtooth* (2009) for Yorgos Lanthimos.

Constantine Giannaris
FROM THE EDGE OF THE CITY
1997

In the background, Athens is in the midst of reconstruction and growth as the city prepares for the 2004 Olympics; in the foreground, a group of young immigrants from Russia try to make ends meet, struggle with alienation and marginalisation, turn to prostitution and tell their stories. A Greek, much more politicised version of *My Own Private Idaho* that left its mark on 1990s Greece.

Panos Koutras
XENIA
2014

From the director of the acclaimed films *Attack of the Giant Moussaka* (1999) and *Strella* (2009), *Xenia* is the story of two young Greek-Albanian men who embark on an odyssey in the hope of finding their Greek father, who has been missing for some time and who they suspect has become a neo-fascist politician. A political film on sexual and national identity, alternative relationships and communities, queer dreams and love.

'It appears that a new generation of filmmakers considers this whole story of Weird Greek Cinema to be a source on which they can rely for international recognition while at the same time wondering how they can break free of it.'

the label Greek Weird Wave international TV subscription channels host special seasons, books are written and dedicated nights are organised at festivals and in film archives.

It might even be that the idea of a weird Greek cinema that does not want to forgo the generous international reception it often receives has become a self-reflexive allusion in recent films, such as Babis Makridis's *Pity* (2018), scripted by Efthimis Filippou, in which the central character becomes so used to the pity he receives because his spouse is in a coma that, when she unexpectedly recovers, he decides to kill her along with the rest of the family.

It also appears that a new generation of filmmakers considers this whole story of Weird Greek Cinema to be a source on which they can rely for international recognition while at the same time wondering how they can break free of it – this, for example, is a way of reading the worthwhile short, mid- and feature-length films of younger Greek directors such as Konstantina Gotzamani, Jacqueline Lentzou, Yorgos Zois, Zachary Mavroidis and Christos Massalas.

*

In one of the more enjoyable Greek movies of recent times, *Suntan* by Argyris Papadimitropoulos (2016), Makis Papadimitriou (the actor in the video we discussed earlier) plays a doctor who, driven by unemployment and some professional issues, decides to move to the small picturesque island of Antiparos. In winter the locals are on their own and almost nothing happens; in summer, however, the island fills up. Tourists of all ages, but especially young ones, come from all over the world to this small earthly paradise to acquire the suntan of the title in exchange for providing the developmental fuel this small society needs for its survival. The doctor – strange, trapped, a loser hiding a secret from his past – spends his first winter quietly, but in the summer everything suddenly turns upside down. He falls in love with a female tourist. He is all at sea. He follows groups of holidaymakers around, not knowing how to behave and how to make himself liked. He is the odd one out in the group (and often the butt of its jokes) – someone we might consider a bit weird. He is also the one who wants to extricate himself from his day-to-day reality, even if only by dreaming. From the middle of the film onwards, what we are watching could be him dreaming or a surrealist epilogue playing with the film's genre. The doctor, in a frenzy after wandering the island (the viewer witnesses the most unedifying scenes of partying tourists on a Greek island in August), abducts the girl he 'loves', drugs her and takes her to his surgery. The film ends with him standing over her, surveying her body as he had when he first encountered her, once again as a doctor. The film's comic effect comes not just from the main character perceiving himself differently from the way others see him, it is much more to do with the fact that, after a certain point, the viewer begins to see the film as a metaphor, as more or less a self-referential allegory. The comedy in *Suntan* works because the film is also a commentary – not only on the representation of Greece as a 'summertime paradise' but also on every Greek film that doesn't know quite how to play around with genre, and which genre to play with, but tries to get results by means of excess and amateurish mix-ups. The doctor's character also in a way mirrors recent Greek cinema itself insofar as it understands that others elsewhere often see it as the village oddball. Surrealist cinema ends up offering an indirectly illuminating picture of what is happening in the country; and a collection of scenes that might even be seen as completely realistic end up convincing you that you should perceive them as ironic allegories.

The story of recent Weird Greek Cinema, which started with a family whose members abused one another within the constraints of four walls, could end here, in a doctor's surgery with a woman's body lying on the examination table and a strange, frenzied man looking down at her, with the viewer uncertain how far the irony goes (and what its target is) and whether the social critique that might be at play (including the portrayal of gender-related violence) is meant seriously or is just another ironic pirouette. You might think that this is a weird movie that doesn't know how to finish – or, even, how to take responsibility for what it is trying to say, that you are watching a private joke about splatter movies, that gender-related violence and its representation are made the objects of satire (and not in a particularly politically correct manner) but also that, suddenly, what you are seeing is a hilarious, albeit somewhat shallow, send-up of every speech about 'love', 'salvation', 'development'

and 'reparation' that Greeks have had to endure in the last few years.

Greek cinema appears in recent times to have expressed, often in ways that are not straightforward and certainly not always realistic, a latent violence, an erosion of institutions and traditional systems of identity and community (such as the family), an intolerance of the old reference systems (including older Greek cinema and its iconography), a tendency to revise one's way of talking about a contemporary reality in crisis, a propensity to engage again with an international audience and a set of questions about how it might achieve this. As in the final scene of *Suntan*, and as we are reminded by the video from the Greek Association of Film Producers-Directors I mentioned at the start, Greek cinema is still left with a different set of questions that it needs to answer, questions concerning its political stance, its next steps, its funding and the audience it targets. Last but not least there is what lies behind the question of who will give it 'a little love', how this cinema will move on to transform a frenzy of mobility and critical overdrive into a more emotionally focused engagement. 🖎

The Greek Freak:

Giannis Antetokounmpo

THOMAS TSALAPATIS
Translated by Konstantine Matsoukas

There is something miraculous about the achievements of this basketball star of Nigerian descent, on both a sporting and a human level, and his exploits have even forced the far right in Greece to backpedal and agree to grant him citizenship.

and the Road
to Heaven

Giannis Antetokounmpo – the son of migrants from Nigeria – who, at sixteen, started out selling watches and sunglasses at traffic intersections in Athens is now, at twenty-five, the recipient of the NBA's MVP (Most Valuable Player) award for the 2018–19 season. His story is like a fairy tale, like one of those impossibly optimistic Hollywood films in which, through the protagonist's self-belief and persistence in the face of adversity, it all comes out right in the end. Television specials, articles in sports magazines and newspapers the world over tell the story of the 'Greek Freak', his humble origins, his meteoric rise to the top. And here, in Greece, we have learned to be enthusiastic about the unexpected, about this kid who came from nowhere and is heading towards always and everywhere, overcoming every obstacle, driving new roads into uncharted territories. There are some who do not believe this young man fits their idea of what a Greek should be, but they can't help identifying with him and rejoicing in his successes on a personal level. A compromise has been reached that overcomes prejudices, fixations and stereotypes, one born not so much out of Giannis Antetokounmpo's successes as of the wonderful style of his game, the speed that sweeps everything along, his body leaning into an endless 'Forward', the combination of muscle, skill and imagination coming together to turn a sporting event into art. In front of these images there can

be no footnotes, second thoughts or objections. Here the body is music.

The recent history of Greek basketball is one of those rare collective stories of expectation and success in the country. And I don't just mean in sport. The story of Giannis Antetokounmpo is not just about Greek basketball. It starts with what is left out, on the margins of Greek society. And that is why it is the only story that can show this society in its entirety. Including its margins. It captures a moment of Greek society's reconciliation with itself.

THE GAME IN THIS PART OF THE WORLD

Somewhere on a basketball court in Athens around the beginning or the end of the 1990s, a misshaped hoop without a net and a worn-out cassette player with only one working speaker. We hardly knew any NBA players – most of those we could name were from stickers; we did know a few Europeans, but they didn't have the same legendary status. While you lined up for a shot you whispered their names, because for one moment you were them as you waited for the ball to drop through the hoop, and we only understood a few verses of grunge and rock ('foreign songs' as they were called by those who didn't like us), a few verses because most of the words in them were not taught in the after-school English class, and anyway, we'd skipped the lesson so we could play basketball. An age full of spelling mistakes, playing truant, avoiding that insufferable guy who sounded like our parents and wagged his finger at us like

THOMAS TSALAPATIS is a poet, playwright and journalist who regularly writes for a number of Greek publications. His first collection, *Ximeroma inai sfayi Kirie Krak* ('The Dawn Kills, Mr Krak') is an innovative alternation of prose and poetry that won him the National Literary Award in Greece for best new writer.

the head teacher. And for as long as the riffs kept up you were free, and getting up early in the morning was the furthest thing from your mind …

'Feta cheese, Nikos Galis and poets.' That is the answer with which I used to start the poetry seminars I gave to schoolchildren. The question behind the answer was a simple one: 'What does Greece produce?' Certainly, the question is a great deal more knowing than its phrasing suggests – especially because it was asked to elicit the answer 'Nothing'. It was one of the principal arguments put forward by both the 'lenders' to the Greek economy and their local mouthpieces, the politicians and journalists who espoused a never-ending austerity, a range of cutbacks in jobs and employment rights. The belief that the country had ceased to create primary wealth and was living off services, tourism and loans. On this was built the myth of the lazy Greek and, by extension, the lazy southern European. My answer expressed a proud – and slightly smartass – attitude with regard to the narrative that describes a whole people (the Greeks in this case) as lazy and useless, as being entirely responsible for all the ills that befell them during the crisis. In fact, the question was no more than a stratagem for me to win the kids over to poetry and poets by linking them with basketball. The beginning of a conversation that would continue over several sessions.

As I revisit that answer today, I find it still rings true. But it's not the feta cheese that grabs my attention. And the subject of poetry is for a different discussion. My thoughts are arrested by Nikos Galis. Perhaps the greatest athlete of the last century, Nikos Galis *is* Greek basketball. What's more, he is what sets Greek basketball apart from all other team sports. A silent figure with a great talent and an even greater work ethic. The man who managed to convince the generations of kids who saw him play (and the ones that followed them) to take up basketball. The man who won the 1987 FIBA EuroBasket, who was, until recently, the top scorer in the game's history and who, in 2017, was inducted into the Naismith Memorial Basketball Hall of Fame.

Before 1987 those who preferred basketball to football were few and far between. Today, while football remains the top sport, basketball comes a close second. More to the point, there is the realisation that good Greek basketball players really do exist, players who can hold their own on any basketball court in the world. In contrast to the middling standard of most Greek footballers, Greek basketball players can take their places at the top table of international basketball – proof of this being the second EuroBasket that Greece won in 2005, the 2006 victory over the USA in the World Cup semi-finals in Saitama, Japan, the European championships of Panathinaikos and Olympiakos, the careers of Greek basketball greats Vassilis Spanoulis, Theodoros Papaloukas and Dimitris Diamandidis.

It is fair to say that Greek basketball seems to tie in with many different aspects of Greek reality. Let us consider the urbanisation and spread of Athens in recent decades. In the 1960s and 1970s the capital's population soared as more and more families relocated from rural areas in search of work. The apartment blocks built to house this growing population covered over the city's empty spaces, the vacant plots on which previous generations had learned to play football. Today it is easier to find a basketball hoop than football goalposts in Athens. Every neighbourhood has its own small court. It is in one of those, in the Sepolia district, that Giannis

Antetokounmpo played his first games.

His parents had come to Greece from Lagos, Nigeria, in 1991, three years before his birth. Even though Antetokounmpo and his three brothers were born and raised in Greece, they did not automatically acquire Greek nationality. Up to the age of eighteen Antetokounmpo had no official papers and was a citizen of neither Greece nor Nigeria. Until recently the children of migrants born in Greece were ghosts. They were not granted the nationality of their country of origin; our country turned its back on them.

IDENTITY AS REWARD

You imitated the stars and whispered their names wrong but emulated their celebrations perfectly. Barkley, Kevin Johnson, and I swear that I don't have a gun, Horace Grant, Penny Hardaway, you want it all but you can't have it, it's in your face but you can't grab it, Predrag Danilović, Stojko Vranković, this is what you get when you mess with us, a random mix, irregular, but always reflecting our mood with its lack of order. Every song told the truth so long as it didn't remind you of what oppressed you and smothered you. And you sweated not to find your way in this tough life (what crap) but just to feel alive ...

'I want to thank you and tell you how moved we have been; all Greeks have seen how you have fought since you were young, helping your brothers and becoming a role model to many. And I want to say one more thing – and I say this with real emotion because it is how I feel – I hope you drive them crazy in the States with your dunking! Be well, be strong. And I want you to know that this is a happy day for all of us watching you; the whole country is there for you. Thank you for flying the flag with your brother. You showed them a little bit of Greece out there.' With these words the then prime minister, Antonis Samaras,

The Greek national basketball team achieved one of their most memorable victories on 1 September 2006, at the semi-finals of the men's World Championship, which was being played that year in Japan. The United States met Greece for a place in the final in Saitama, and the result seemed a foregone conclusion: the US team, coached by Mike Krzyzewski, featured numerous champions and the NBA's best players, including Carmelo Anthony, Dwyane Wade and a young LeBron James. And yet 15.6 seconds from the end of the match (in basketball, even tenths of a second are important), the crowd could not believe their eyes: Michalis Kakiouzis, a Greek forward who played for Barcelona, had just pulled off two free throws to put the Greeks 101-95 up. In the few remaining seconds both LeBron James and Chris Paul tried to narrow the gap with two three-point shots, but each time the ball hit the rim. Theodoros Papaloukas took the rebound and ran towards the opposition's basket, waiting for the final whistle, then released the tension by kicking the ball into the stands. Time was up, and Greece were in the final. On 3 September, however, it was Spain's turn to celebrate with a crushing victory, but that is another story ... Greece still had the silver medal and their best ever result at the World Championship.

'The story of the Greek Freak ought to be a permanent reminder of the difficulties migrants face within Greece and throughout Europe.'

wished Giannis Antetokounmpo well at the Athens Concert Hall, to which he had invited Antetokounmpo to celebrate his achievements. These words would have been little more than the usual platitudes had they not been hypocritical to the point of mockery. The Samaras government was the country's most conservative since the dictatorship. During his term the authorities treated refugees and migrants like so much human garbage. In his speeches Samaras made constant reference to the 'threat of illegal migration', identified migrants collectively with terrorism and frequently gave vent to populist racism with statements such as, 'Migrants have filled all the nursery schools, and Greeks can no longer find places for their children. This must end.'

The disparity between the two statements demonstrates a level of hypocrisy that borders on schizophrenia. Let us consider what it is that Antetokounmpo has fought against ever since he was a child, as Samaras mentioned: against the conditions faced daily by those on the receiving end of the government's migration policy, against hate speech in public statements, against the government fertiliser that nurtured the thorns of the extreme-right Golden Dawn.

More to the point, however, the inconsistency between the two statements is indicative of the terms in which the institutions of power in Greece – and elsewhere – understand and manage identity. Identity is a reward for being functional, for being useful. It is not a state of being, a fact of existence, a right to self-definition.

It is merely a method of segregation. Let us think of identity in reverse and separated from nationality; let us think about gender, sexual choice, aesthetics, moral or political positions. If you are not deemed functional according to the priorities of certain institutions you are stripped of all definition, every aspect of identity is removed and your existence ends up being something relative. In the Greece of prime ministers driven crazy by basketball dunks, if you are HIV-positive, homosexual, homeless, an anarchist or any number of other things, your allotted place of residence is an anonymous no man's land: the wire fence of Evros on the Greek–Turkish border or the bottom of the Aegean.

Giannis Antetokounmpo had the luck to be born with a rare talent. So rare that it forced even members of the then governing extreme right to look the other way, fearing the international outcry (which had already begun), and grant him nationality. The story of the Greek Freak ought to be a permanent reminder of the difficulties migrants face within Greece and throughout Europe.

THE FREAK

On these courts time is so fleeting that it all but evaporates, and dreams are never dreams but lived experiences, they fill basketball courts and concert halls at the same time, in a future vast and instantaneous, intangible and perfectly specific. And you were both Michael Jordan and Kurt Cobain, for as long as a song or a poorly coordinated attack lasted. Although you were getting older, you kept tripping over your shoelaces. Here are

*the young men, the weight on their shoulders,
here are the young men, well, where have they
been …*

The story of a Greek-Nigerian who managed, in the space of five years, to go from the obscure minor league of Greek basketball to become the symbol of a team and a city, a franchise player for the Milwaukee Bucks and an MVP seems almost to defy logic in favour of the optimistic plotlines of a soap opera, a fairy tale, as if it were beyond explanation. As I write these lines the Bucks are top of the NBA, tickets to their games are nigh on impossible to get hold of and they are building a new arena with a larger capacity. Shops and restaurants are springing up around the arena, new jobs being created – and this whole upbeat narrative has the name of the Greek Freak written all over it. Most importantly, the journey to this place can be followed, easily traceable, step by step, conquest after conquest.

To the rest of the world Antetokounmpo may be the NBA's 'Next Big Thing', a player who redefines the rules of the game. At a time that large-bodied centre players are being eclipsed by the speed and accuracy of shorter guards, Giannis's game moves in exactly the opposite direction. A player whose build allows him to play in any position, he is today the tallest guard in NBA history. While other guards will rely on the three-point field goal, he will counter with infiltration and the element of surprise. Similar in height to Magic Johnson and in explosiveness to LeBron James, Giannis is already a basketball phenomenon.

But for us, here in Greece, he is much more. He is a man who managed to encapsulate the contradictions of a whole society and move them in a positive direction. Without making statements or issuing manifestos but simply by his example, simply through his beautiful game. A society

BASKETBALL ULTRAS

Greek basketball and football teams often have two things in common: their names (most clubs field teams in multiple sports) and their fiery supporters. Basketball fans are no less passionate than their football counterparts, and the support is some of the most fervent in the world, particularly when it comes to the mother of all clashes: the derby between the Greens of Panathinaikos, who once represented the wealthy, conservative class, and the Reds of Olympiakos, the working-class team from Piraeus. Anything can happen at these games: from the 2017 final suspended because smoke bombs were being set off to the February 2019 encounter interrupted by the Olympiakos players walking off in protest at the referee's decisions. Irked by this less than chivalrous and 'manly' withdrawal, the chairman of Panathinaikos left a red thong on the bench abandoned by his rivals. Panathinaikos fans, under the umbrella of their historic supporters' union Gate 13, founded in 1966, are famous for their song 'Horto Magiko': 'It's a magical weed/Give me a little taste/So I can dream of my PAO/And shout up to God/My Panatha, I love you/Like heroin, like a hard drug/Like hashish, like LSD/The whole world is high for you, PAO, the whole world.' As with ultras everywhere, many lean to the right politically, but there are also left-wing fans, such as those of Athens club Panionios, who successfully opposed the appointment of coach Steve Giatzoglou, a supporter of Golden Dawn. He did not take it well. 'Of course I'm a fascist,' he said. 'Sport is fascism. What are coaches? None of us has democratic principles. That's how it is. What can you do … ?'

A depiction of Giannis Antetokounmpo on a basketball court in the Sepolia district of Athens where the NBA champion was born and raised.

THE PASSENGER   Thomas Tsalapatis

capable of surprising you, positively or negatively, with its unexpected hospitality or its irrational racism.

For us, here in Greece, maybe he is a major part of our armoury in the fight against daily racism, as one of the fundamental arguments in a discussion that excludes argument. The Nazi leader of the Golden Dawn may have called him an ape and the deputy prime minister of New Democracy may have made mocking remarks about his Greekness, but these racist outbursts don't change anything. In this case the words of the right wingers mean nothing, not even to their followers – not really. Precisely because Antetokounmpo lacks connection with the political sentiments or the fixed views of Greeks, he invades the emotions, generates acceptance; he teaches coexistence through unconditional admiration. He makes racial hypocrisy turn on itself. And even if this betrays a lack of sincerity, in this very insincerity we can smell a victory. When someone tries to gloss over archaic views and beliefs (as did the former prime minister and his acolytes) it is because they realise how out of step those views are. Not only does he recognise the error of his ways (even if he continues to defend it) but his hypocritical stance renders it redundant.

I live in Kypseli, an area of Athens exposed to daily racism of the petty kind. Just stand in the queue at the post office in Kypseli Square any morning, and you'll soon find out what everyday racism is: the comments, the behaviour, the expressions on the faces of this man and that woman. You often feel despair. But, walking on a little further, that despair dissipates. In the squares of Kypseli you see mixed groups of children playing, unconcerned with origin, race, colour and the like. Their coexistence has the naturalness of basketball, of a lay-up with no opposition defenders to

GOLDEN DAWN

Golden Dawn is a neo-fascist organisation founded in 1980 by Nikolaos Michaloliakos, an extremist with a number of convictions for political crimes and violence. It was actually in prison that he met some of those who had ruled Greece between 1967 and 1974 and laid the foundations for the party, which made no secret of being openly neo-Nazi in its early years – in fact, the name of the party derives from the false belief that Hitler was a member of the Hermetic Order of the Golden Dawn, the secret society associated with the British occultist Aleister Crowley and the poet W.B. Yeats. Its cultural and political reference points, besides Greece under the Colonels, are the legend of the civil war against the communists (1946–9) and the dictatorship of Ioannis Metaxas (1936–41). Very active on the ground, they volunteer for social initiatives to support Greek people – acting as bodyguards for pensioners drawing their pension, donating blood, providing medical assistance for the homeless – whereas their anti-immigration line often escalates from words into deeds: indiscriminate attacks on immigrants are the order of the day. Golden Dawn's fortress is the Mani region, the southern point of the Peloponnese and a symbol of resistance to Ottoman domination, which is a source of pride for the hot-blooded inhabitants of an area still bypassed by development. The party began to attract attention in the 1990s when the Macedonian question flared up (see 'North Macedonia' on page 88) and, despite a long string of court cases involving its leaders – notably after the murder of the anti-fascist rapper Pavlos Fyssas in 2013 – it continues to grow in popularity.

'And the real question is, could you ever be a supporter of the far right if you've grown up with Antetokounmpo's name on your back?'

block you. It is these kids and the many others like them who will grow up wearing the singlet of a player with a Greek first name and a Nigerian surname.

And the real question is, could you ever be a supporter of the far right if you've grown up with Antetokounmpo's name on your back?

BASKETBALL AS ART AND AS HOPE

And today you are over thirty, listening to the same music, and no player will ever move you like Bodiroga, your song just as off-key as your three-pointer, none of us played in the NBA, none of us got a record out, one of us, the tallest, today teaches at a conservatory.

I don't know if I, too, am influenced by Giannis's forward charge, but I believe there is something at the very core of basketball that can make you feel optimistic. A system of cooperation and exchange capable of implementing change.

Of all team sports, basketball is the most collective, with a series of strategies and combinations that keep evolving. Cooperation is at its core. Not as a moral requirement but as a prerequisite for good play. There has never been a team that got anywhere by relying on one player alone. Even Wilt Chamberlain – the only player ever to score one hundred points in a single NBA game – although he excelled in every category, could never top the team spirit of Bill Russell and the Boston Celtics, the very model of teamwork in the 1950s and 1960s. Success has always included the socialism of the pass, the work of many hands.

You might at first be excited by the skill of an individual performance, a player's accuracy or the spectacle of a dunk, but really it's all about the passing, how the players move off the ball, the silent alignments and lines created in space. What heightens the sensation is the limitations. The space made smaller by the opposition's defence as well as the constraints of the court; time shrunk by stopwatches and the rhythm of play. Every performance becomes a collective achievement in the face of what the opposition tries to take away from you. The planning and inspiration of one become a map for the many, and the outcome is an act of synergy whose simple success we rarely encounter in other areas of daily life. The history of a passion is always written in the same way, from the first successful ten seconds of a coordinated effort by a group of friends on some godforsaken court to championship games in the gleaming arenas of Europe or the United States. It is the passing that shows what a team is worth, that makes sticking to the rules a source of liberation and inspiration.

Through the transient, short-lived spectacle we may be able to capture that rare feeling, a childlike enthusiasm that judges not with rigour but with sincerity. The smile as we watch a crossover dribble by James Harden, a shot by LeBron James or an offensive play by Giannis Antetokounmpo. Above all, the joy in success through cooperative endeavour, whatever the outcome. 🏃

David and Goliath

GILDA TENTORIO

Translated by Alan Thawley

Most of the time, imagination has to come to terms with reality, but sometimes the opposite occurs. That is what happened in Greece in the 1990s, in a dispute between a Greek writer and one of the world's most powerful multinationals.

The author in question was Eugene Trivizas (born 1946), who is also a lecturer in criminology in the UK at the University of Reading and who has worked with Scotland Yard in London. But rather than being a writer of crime fiction or a serious academic – as might be expected from his day job – Trivizas is a children's author with more than 150 books to his name, many of which have also been turned into plays and musicals. His writing is appreciated by old and young alike, with its enchanting, sparkling language full of puns that can present even the most expert translators with a challenge.

Among his characters are fearless, rebellious heroes: the scarecrow who wants to take to the skies with his bird friends, the snowman who sets off for the North Pole to avoid melting, the mice who take on the cats and win … They come from places called Piperu, the Island of Fireworks and the Province of All Colours Except Pink, but the most famous place is Fruitopia, a utopian city inhabited by – you've guessed it – apples, strawberries, tomatoes and all kinds of other fruits and vegetables. After suffering years of injustice and torture at the hands of unscrupulous greengrocers who froze, cooked, cut up, squeezed or blended them, they finally rose up and overthrew the tyrannical regime, transforming Fruitopia into a democratic republic with a president, a constitution and two football teams. As a reflection of the real world, the vegetable community faces conflicts, jealousies and hunger for power and also sets up its own army to fend off attacks from shady characters and foreign businesses who want to get their hands on their city. In other words, drama is guaranteed on every page.

But this is more than just an entertaining parable to make us think about political and environmental issues. The world invented by Eugene Trivizas still inspires a sense of pride and a certain patriotism in Greek people: in 1994 Coca-Cola launched a new drink on the American and Australian markets aimed at teenagers. Its name was Fruitopia. Sound familiar? The drink was an instant success: Fruitopia earned a place in *Time* magazine's top-ten products of the year and was even mentioned in an episode of *The Simpsons*. But when preparations were being made for the drink to conquer the European – and therefore Greek – markets, Coca-Cola had not reckoned with Trivizas, who decided to take legal action to defend his intellectual property. You might think that it would have been a lost cause from the off, but, in a historic verdict, the court ruled in his favour, forcing the multinational to beat a retreat. An unexpected happy ending: little David defeated the giant Goliath, the fruit utopia defeated the American colossus, showing that Greek imagination is a winning brand.

Tales from Another Greece

The Parthenon of Nashville is a landmark in the US city. It stands on top of a hill in Centennial Park, by the lake with ducks swimming on it. The park was the setting for the 1897 celebrations of the centenary of the state of Tennessee. That year, a six-month programme of events and record-breaking celebrations were held at the park and the Parthenon. There were performances of Greek tragedies and exhibitions of medical marvels such as radiography, which was demonstrated by taking X-rays of the hands of a governor and other dignitaries, as well as what the posters proclaimed at the time to be 'the largest firework display ever seen in Nashville'. With its motto 'Nashville, the Athens of the South', the city was the cradle of a transplanted ideal of Greek culture, having been the first city in the USA to set up a publicly funded school system. During a visit to the centenary celebrations, a senator from Ohio, W.T. Clarke, declared that Nashville had 'the largest scholastic population in any city in the country; four female seminaries; three colleges for the education of the colored people, including Fisk University, the singers of which have established a worldwide reputation. Vanderbilt University, with her endowment of over a million dollars, three medical schools, three schools of pharmacy, two law schools, three large dental schools.' Like other buildings constructed exclusively for the centenary, the Parthenon was designed as a temporary structure, but the locals grew to like it and decided to fight the ravages of time. By 1920 the cheap materials with which it had been constructed began to imitate the dilapidation of the original temple, so the structure was rebuilt and fully reopened to the public in 1931. The idea of re-creating the Parthenon came from Eugene Castner Lewis, director of exhibitions for the Tennessee centenary, described by newspapers in the late nineteenth century as 'a little man, slender and unassuming', but also as 'a dreamer but one who tended to make dreams a reality'. Lewis is now buried in the city's cemetery in a mausoleum in the shape of a miniature Egyptian pyramid, guarded on either side by two little sphinxes. The Nashville Parthenon, on the other hand, is the only life-sized copy in the world. Inside stands

VALERIO MILLEFOGLIE
Translated by Alan Thawley

a replica of Phidias' statue of the goddess Athena, thirteen metres high and covered entirely in gold. Dedicated to the suffragette movement, it was commissioned from the sculptor Alan LeQuire in 1982 and delivered in 1990. What is missing from the original temple is present in Nashville, including plaster casts of the marbles controversially taken by Lord Elgin in 1801 and held by the British Museum in London. (On 26 January 2019, in an interview published by the Greek newspaper *Ta Nea*, Hartwig Fischer, director of the museum, rejected a return of the sculptures, which had been requested by the new Acropolis Museum in Athens, stating that their removal had been a 'creative act' rather than a theft.) In the park is another artwork by LeQuire, a memorial to Anne Dallas Dudley, founder of the Nashville Equal Suffrage League, who, on 20 February 1913, said on the subject of extending voting rights to women, 'This is a government of, for, and by the people, and only the law denies that women are people.' In the final scene of Robert Altman's film *Nashville*, country star Barbara Jean, played by Ronee Blakley, is assassinated while singing 'My Idaho Home' on the steps of the Parthenon during a presidential candidate's campaign. In 2006 the solo electronic music artist

Casiotone for the Painfully Alone released the song 'Nashville Parthenon'. Those who visited at Christmas between 1954 and 1967 would have been able to admire it as the backdrop to a large nativity scene presented by a department-store chain. On 18 July 1961 six African-Americans attempted to dive into the park's communal swimming pool under the impression that, as tax-paying residents, it was their property. They were thrown out. On 16 April 1982 Kevin Longinotti, a student at Vanderbilt University, was picnicking in the park with other friends from the university when a powerful tornado broke the branches of a number of ancient trees and buried him for forty-five minutes. He died three weeks later in hospital. A dark seascape with lights cutting through the sky, leaving the wreck of a ship in the shadows: this is one of the sixty-three oil paintings in the Parthenon's permanent collection, most of them landscapes, all by American artists, donated by the insurance executive and collector James M. Cowan. In 1927 he said, 'It will be my hope that what has given me pleasure in collecting and studying for a great portion of my life, may prove to be of permanent benefit to the friends and citizens and coming generations of the state I love above all others.'

An Author Recommends

A book, a film and an album to understand Greece, chosen by:

ERSI SOTIROPOULOS
Translated by Alan Thawley

Ersi Sotiropoulos is the author of a wealth of poems, short stories and novels that have received numerous awards and been translated into English, French, German, Spanish, Italian, Turkish and Swedish. The French edition of *What's Left of the Night* (published in English by New Vessel Press in 2018) was nominated for the European Book Prize, shortlisted for the Prix Femina and won the Prix Méditerranée Étranger in 2017.

THE BOOK
THEIR SMELL MAKES ME WANT TO CRY
Menis Koumandareas
University of Birmingham
2007

I would have preferred to recommend another book by this great writer and dear friend of mine, who was found murdered in his apartment in December 2014. To my mind, his novel *O Oraios Lochagos* ('The Handsome Captain') is his masterpiece, but unfortunately it has only been translated into French and German. Menis Koumandareas was the Athenian writer *par excellence*: Athens becomes a protagonist in his books, a city both remote and present, archaic and futuristic, suffocating and pierced by rays of light that every so often allow a casual gesture of affection or some furtive body contact to occur. *Their Smell Makes Me Want to Cry*, published in Greece in 1996, is a series of stories told by Euripides, a barber in Athens who listens closely to his customers' stories because, as he says, 'it helps with cutting their hair and it lightens their souls'. Stories of loneliness, of absurd moments, of a typical Greek surrealism that never becomes implausible. A doctor named Death, a cat in the arms of a sailor, a motorbike with a headless rider: all of these figure in an Athenian mythology that cuts across time, sometimes leaving a sense of estrangement like a momentary distancing effect that serves to sharpen the focus. With virtuoso skill, in simple, seemingly unrefined language and with no recourse to literary artifice, *Their Smell Makes Me Want to Cry* speaks to us of what is happening around us at all times, transforming our everyday surroundings into art.

THE FILM
STRELLA (a.k.a. A WOMAN'S WAY)
Panos Koutras
2009

The Athens of dirty streets where Strella walks, the Athens of slums where tenants kill time with coffee, cigarettes, whisky and sometimes drugs, is, ultimately, a friendly city. A world that has suffered for generations, but remains joyful at heart, breathes in these anonymous neighbourhoods and miraculously survives, always on the cusp of tragedy, yet burning only the tips of its wings. 'Don't go. We'll make it,' says the father/lover to his transvestite son. Like in an ancient tragedy. But this time it is the androgyne who throws in the towel, revealing his double identity in all its splendour. The idyll begins like all idylls: with glances, little acts and gifts. Several times a squirrel interrupts the plot, seemingly innocuous, surrounded by a green landscape, but then bares its teeth menacingly. There is a whole range of possible love choices in this film, and, at the same time, everyone is in a hurry to rid themselves of any sense of guilt. Unlike dramas from northern countries with their long silences, those from the Mediterranean carry the hope of forgiveness, not just because of the outlet provided by the arguments and fights but also because it draws on the deep reservoir of compassion held by those who have been abandoned. Thus, the modest house can be transformed into a temple of tender love, a temple where everyone is welcome – kids and old men, incestuous lovers, transvestites, ex-convicts and drug dealers – in a kindly, kitschy atmosphere with mechanical toys and multi-coloured lanterns. How will the story end? Will the heroes be able to find their way, or will they be devoured, victims of a fate beyond their control? The film leaves the question open. The first step is reconciliation.

THE ALBUM
PROSKLISI SE DEIPNO KYANIOU ('INVITATION TO A CYANIDE DINNER')
Thanasis Papakonstantinou
2014

In the wake of those three Greek musical greats, Mikis Theodorakis, Manos Hatzidakis and Dionysis Savvopoulos (the latter pioneering a combination of rock with rebetiko and introducing strong, original verses), the Greek music scene appeared to be quite confused, stagnant, overshadowed by pop and the omnipresent light music of the bouzouki clubs. But the crisis seems to have become a breeding ground for new experimentation in a number of directions: new groups and singer-songwriters emerged, some disappearing before we even got to hear from them. Among the pioneers, Thanasis Papakonstantinou, who was already known before the crisis, came to the audience's attention primarily thanks to his exceptional 2006 album, *I vrochi apo kato* ('The Rain from Below'), which immediately earned him a devoted fan base. Papakonstantinou experiments with a mix of West and East (similar experimentation, but on a different level, could be heard in Latinitas Nostra's magnificent performance *A Voyage into the Levant* at the 2013 Athens Festival, which combined Baroque and Eastern music: 'Lachrimae' by the Elizabethan composer John Dowland with Ottoman *amanedes*). The album *Prosklisi se deipno kyaniou* ('Invitation to a Cyanide Dinner') has its roots in traditional music, rebetiko and folk, with forays into rock and psychedelia; it ranges widely but remains a cohesive whole. Papakonstantinou creates his own world by using word association and drawing inspiration from poetry, recounting stories of everyday life, always with an element of paradox – as in the beautiful 'Iliopetra' ('Sun Stone'), in which he achieves a combination of intimate tone and collective feelings.

The Playlist

Listen to this playlist at:
open.spotify.com/user/iperborea

KONSTANTINOS FRAGKOULIS
Translated by Konstantine Matsoukas

Twelve very different contemporary Greek singers, composers and poets – like the twelve gods of Olympus. Men and women who never put down their instruments, they shout, laugh and cry behind their screens in their home recording studios. Millions of romantic, melancholic lovers of light whose brains seem fried by the sun, by interwar poetry or a rave next door to a run-down cinema. Contemporary Greek music, inspired by the East, by 1980s punk and electro, wants to dance but also to confront us in a smoky basement then, at the end of the evening, drunk on a public bench, declare its undying love as dawn rises.

Greek music in the 1990s takes in electronic music and alternative rock groups, usually with English names and English lyrics. The culture clash between rock and disco is over now, and music seems to be looking for a new direction. Folk music becomes more arty and, while still following tradition, mixes it up with other musical genres. Musicians are now under the spell of a beat, inspired by Bristol's trip-hop scene, as well as grunge from Seattle. An introverted and mightily pissed-off generation is coming into its own ...

Greek musicians travel playing cello, bouzouki or hip-hop loops on a drum machine. They listen to the radio and read music magazines that give away free CDs. They pack the live music venues every Monday night and then go straight to work, thoughtful, seduced by the angst and torment that come with any great love.

1

Felizol
& The Boy
'Mia fora'
2017

2

Thanasis
Papakonstantinou
'Agrypnia'
2002

3

Savina
Yannatou
'I pedias kai to
nekrotafion'
1982

4

Giannis Aggelakas
& Nikos Veliotis
'Opos xypnoun
oi erastes'
2007

5

Avaton
'Aloessa'
1995

6

Xylina Spathia
'Sto vracho'
1997

7

Ichotopia
'Thalassa'
2017

8

Diafana Krina
'Meres argias'
1996

9

Lena Platonos
'Ematines
skies apo
apostasi'
2015

10

Stereo Nova
'To puzzle
ston aera'
1993

11

Nikos
Papazoglou
'Chtes to vradi'
1984

12

Mode Plagal
'Emena mou to
'pan ta poulia'
2001

Further Reading

FICTION

David Connolly (ed.)
Angelic & Black: Contemporary Greek Short Stories
Attica Editions, 2006

Rhea Galanaki
I Shall Sign as Loui
Northwestern University Press, 2000

Christos Ikonomou
Something Will Happen, You'll See
Archipelago, 2016

Ioanna Karystiani
Back to Delphi
Europa Editions, 2013

Menis Kumandarea
Their Smell Makes Me Want to Cry
University of Birmingham, 2007

Petros Markaris
Zone Defence
Vintage, 2011

Pavlos Matesis
The Daughter
Arcadia, 2010

Ersi Sotiropoulos
What's Left of the Night
New Vessel Press, 2018

Thanassis Valtinos
Orthokosta: A Novel
Yale University Press, 2016

Alki Zei
Wildcat Under Glass
Angelica Vouloumanou/Bookboom, 2015

NON-FICTION

Roberto Calasso
The Marriage of Cadmus and Harmony
Penguin, 2019 (UK) / Vintage, 1994 (USA)

Gail Holst
Road to Rembetika: Music of a Greek Sub-
culture – Songs of Love, Sorrow and Hashish
Denise Harvey, 2014 (revised edition)

Diane Kochilas
Ikaria: Lessons on Food, Life,
and Longevity from the Greek Island
Where People Forget to Die
Rodale Books, 2014

Rory MacLean
Falling for Icarus: A Journey
Among the Cretans
Tauris Parke Paperbacks, 2011

Andrea Marcolongo
The Ingenious Language: Nine
Epic Reasons to Love Greek
Europa Editions, 2019

Mark Mazower
Salonica, City of Ghosts: Christians,
Muslims and Jews 1430–1950
Harper Perennial, 2005 (UK) /
Vintage, 2006 (USA)

Yannis Palaiologos
The 13th Labour of Hercules:
Inside the Greek Crisis
Granta Books, 2015

Yanis Varoufakis
Adults in the Room: My Battle
with Europe's Deep Establishment
Vintage, 2018 (UK) / Farrar, Straus
and Giroux, 2018 (USA) (revised edition)

POETRY

Peter Bien, Peter Constantine, Edmund
Keeley, Karen Van Dyck (eds)
A Century of Greek Poetry: 1900–2000
Attica Editions, 2004

Constantine Cavafy
Complete Poems
William Collins, 2014 (UK) /
Alfred A. Knopf, 2009 (USA)

Theodoros Chiotis (ed.)
Futures: Poetry of the Greek Crisis
Penned in the Margins, 2015

Kiki Dimoula
The Brazen Plagiarist: Selected Poems
Yale University Press, 2014

Odysseas Elytis
Eros, Eros, Eros: Selected & Last Poems
Copper Canyon Press, 1997

Michalis Ganas
A Greek Ballad: Selected Poems
Yale University Press, 2019

Yannis Ritsos
Poems
Libros Libertad, 2018

George Seferis
Complete Poems
Carcanet, 2018

Graphic design and art direction: Tomo Tomo and Pietro Buffa

Photography: Pietro Masturzo
The photographic content is curated by Prospekt Photographers.

Illustrations: Edoardo Massa

Infographics and cartography: Pietro Buffa

Thanks to: Evangelia Avloniti, Kyriakì Boulassidou,
Elisabetta Garieri, Andrea Gessner, Krystalli Glyniadaki,
Maria Frangoulis, Yianni Litovchenko, Thomas Mamakos,
Beatrice Martelli, Dimitris Michalakis, Giorgos Moutafis,
Matteo Nucci, Natassa Papanikolaou, Marcella Petriglia,
Gilda Tentorio, Matteo Tognocchi, Dimitris Tossidis

http://europaeditions.com/thepassenger
http://europaeditions.co.uk/thepassenger
#ThePassengerMag

The Passenger – Greece
© Iperborea S.r.l., Milan, and Europa Editions, 2020

Translators: Konstantine Matsoukas (Greek), Alan Thawley (Italian).
All translations © Iperborea S.r.l., Milan, and Europa Editions, 2020

ISBN: 9781787702189

Printed on Munken Pure thanks to the support of Arctic Paper

Printed by ELCOGRAF S.p.A., Verona, Italy